SHIP'S VALUE

By

KAJ PINEUS, Ph.D., h.c., LL.B.

Maritime Consultant
Gothenburg

SECOND EDITION

|L|L|P|

LONDON NEW YORK HAMBURG HONG KONG
LLOYD'S OF LONDON PRESS LTD.
1986

Lloyd's of London Press Ltd.
Legal Publishing and Conferences Division
26–30 Artillery Lane, London E1 7LX

USA AND CANADA
Lloyd's of London Press Inc.
817 Broadway
New York, NY 10003 U.S.A.

GERMANY
Lloyd's of London Press
PO Box 11 23 47, Deichstrasse 41
2000 Hamburg 11, West Germany

SOUTH EAST ASIA
Lloyd's of London Press (Far East) Ltd.
903 Chung Nam Building
1 Lockhart Road, Wanchai
Hong Kong

British Library Cataloguing in Publication Data
Pineus, Kaj
Ship's value.—2nd ed.
1. Ships—Valuation
I. Title
387.5'1   VM149

ISBN 1-85044-062-X

Text set in 10 on 12pt Baskerville by
Wessex Typesetters, Frome, Somerset
Printed in Great Britain by
St. Edmundsbury Press
Bury St. Edmunds, Suffolk

In memory of my mother
Dagny Arbo Pineus

Contents

	Page
Preface	xi
Acknowledgements	xiii
Table of Cases and Abbreviations Used	xv

1 INTRODUCTION — I

Point of departure	I
Value in the economic sense	I
General observation on course and disposition followed	2
Itinerary	3
Law and legal sources	3
Need of a study of this kind	4

2 VALUES IN GENERAL — 6

Introduction	6
Demarcation lines	6
Market value	7
Dividend value	9
Expectation value	10
Replacement value	10
Utility value	12
Liquidation value	12
Value in respect of ships	13

3 THE TIME ELEMENT — 15.

Introduction	15
Hull Insurance	16
Value for credit purposes	16
Collision recovery	17
Salvage and general average	19
Limitation of liability	19
Other aspects on ship's value	19

4 ASSESSMENT OF SHIP'S VALUE: THE PRACTICAL APPROACH — 20

5 MARKET VALUE   22

Introduction   22
Certificate of valuation   22
The size   23
The type   23
The age   23
Class condition and upkeep   24
Speed   25
Oil consumption   25
Cargo space, loading and discharging gear   26
Refrigerating machinery   26
Cost of newbuilding   26
Specialized vessels   27
Ship's value in damaged condition   28
The market value   28
Restricted market   31
The market value and the charterparty   33

6 INFLUENCE OF THE CHARTERPARTY
ON SHIP'S VALUE   34

Introduction   34
  (a) Does a charterparty influence ship's value to her owner?   34
  (b) Is the number of vessels under charterparty sufficiently large to
       warrant that attention be devoted to the influence of the
       charterparty?   36
  (c) Are charterparties taken into account when assessing ship's
       value?   37
       (i) Situation outside England   37
       (ii) Situation in England   39
       (iii) Situation in the USA   44
  (d) Does the charterparty automatically follow the ship if sold? 45
  (e) The survival of the charterparty in case the ship is sold as a *de
       lega ferenda* problem   46
  (f) Evaluation of the English valuation method   46

7 SHIP'S VALUE FOR CREDIT PURPOSES   47

Introduction   47
Survey of present valuation method used   48
The survival of the charterparty in case the ship is sold as a *de lega
  ferenda* problem   50
  (i) The CMI Conference 1962   50
  (ii) Discussion within the Swedish Maritime Law Committee and
        in the Royal Bill to Parliament   51
Evaluation of present situation   53

8 HULL INSURANCE

Hull insurance and certain valuation problems connected with
  insurance   56
Valued policy. The elements to be taken into account   57
Dual valuation   60
Hull interest, disbursements   61
Discrepancy between value insured and value at time of total loss   64
Unvalued or open policy   67

9 SHIP'S VALUE AS A CLAIM AGAINST COUNTERPARTY IN CASE OF LOSS OWING TO COLLISION

Provisions of law and views of legal writers   75
The CMI Conference 1962   78
Ship's value and loss of profit   80
Effect on distribution of recovery   81
Evaluation of English method of valuation in connection with collision
  claim   83
Application of methods of valuation   84
The situation within the CMI in 1985   85

10 SALVAGE

The pragmatic approach   87
Importance to be attributed to salved values   88
Ship's value after salvage, the pragmatic approach   89
Repairs, the time element   92
How to assess the value of salved ships   92
Chartered vessels, and the Scandinavian view   94
Number of salvage cases dealt with in London   96
Evaluation of the English valuation method in salvage cases   97
Application of method of valuation   100

11 GENERAL AVERAGE

Introduction   101
Place where the voyage ends   103
  (i)   Effect of disrupted market   103
  (ii)   Value at destination as illustrated by old Swedish cases   105
  (iii) Vessel removed from one place to another or immobilized   108
At the termination of the adventure   109
Concluding observations   110

8 HULL INSURANCE — 56

9 SHIP'S VALUE AS A CLAIM AGAINST COUNTERPARTY IN CASE OF LOSS OWING TO COLLISION — 75

10 SALVAGE — 87

11 GENERAL AVERAGE — 101

12 LIMITATION OF LIABILITY

111

Uniformity of the rules — 111
Comparison of the USA and the 1976 Convention limitation system — 111
". . . the interest of such owner in such vessel" — 113
Evaluation of the two systems — 113

13 SUMMARY AND CONCLUSIONS

115

Summary — 115
Conclusions — 117

Bibliography — 119

Index — 123

Preface

The first edition of *Ship's Value* appeared in 1975 as number 52 in the series published by the Gothenburg Maritime Law Association. The Association has kindly allowed me to publish an updated version of the book elsewhere subject to the role of the Gothenburg Maritime Law Association being made clear. I am glad to comply with this request, at the same time signalling that the latest work in their series (by 1985) bears the number 65, no mean achievement for an Association barely 30 years old.

Mr Allen E Schumacher of American Hull Syndicate read a paper on 13 September 1983 before the International Union of Marine Underwriters on the subject "Hull Valuation for Purposes of Insurance." He found *Ship's Value* useful for his purposes and paid high tribute to it.

By then the first edition (distributed *inter alia* to all the members of the Gothenburg Maritime Law Association) was out of print. One of the few spare copies I still had landed in the hands of Mr John E Droeger of Hall Henry Oliver and McRay, San Francisco. With energy and enthusiasm he launched the idea of an updated version being published by Lloyd's of London Press. He prevailed upon Mr Mathew P Vafidis of Lillick, McHose and Charles of San Francisco to come forward with suggestions for an updated version taking into account, among other things, new cases in the USA. This he has done and I am most grateful.

I have greatly benefited from suggestions made, advice given and information obtained from helpful friends. I should like their names to appear, in alphabetical order:
R Brown, L Gorton, P Griggs, B Hellberg, L Lindfelt, H G Mellander, M Nakanishi, L Pettersson, I and J Sandström, R C Sculpher. I thank them all for their help.

For indefatigable help in typing the manuscript I thank G Eklund. A Johnson and R Wesley Lindahl, from two friendly neighbouring offices, have made photocopies exactly when needed.

In the period that has passed since the first edition we have seen major changes in the shipping industry.

Second-hand ships are worth little more than their scrap value of steel when freight rates barely cover operating costs let alone interest payment. World shipping is likely to remain long in the doldrums—perhaps beyond the rest of the decade. The continuing huge imbalance between low demand and potential supply seems to defy ordinary business cycles. *The Economist*, 23 August 1985.

Mark says (2: 22): "And no man putteth new wine into old bottles: else the new wine doth burst the bottles, and the wine is spilled, and the bottles will be marred: but new wine must be put into new bottles".

Wise words, always to remember for an "up-dater".

I have retained my original approach to the subject. I have had to rewrite some parts in view of developments that have taken place; parts of the book I have amplified, parts I have pruned.

A book, updated or not, cannot compete with the Stop Press News of the evening papers. Nor should it. I hope the updated version of *Ship's Value* will nevertheless prove useful.

Gothenburg, 14 December 1985   KAJ PINEUS

Acknowledgements

In October 1973 the University of Gothenburg gave me an Honorary Degree. For this high distinction I felt I owed them a special proof of my appreciation. My friend Kurt Grönfors, Professor of the Law of Transport at Gothenburg University, suggested that I take up the subject *Ship's value* which he thought was very interesting indeed. So did I. I hope the reader will.

The nature of the subject and the regard I owe to my many friends abroad made it natural for me to write in English, particularly so as it will cause no difficulty to the reader in Scandinavia.

There is a French proverb: "Usez de vos amis, mais n'en abusez pas". I have certainly used my friends within the profession, the Comité Maritime International and elsewhere. I am afraid that I have sometimes crossed the borderline set up by the proverb. I want to mention their names here, as a tribute and thank them all for their assistance. I give them in alphabetic order.

H Ameln, Bergen, G Ahrne, Gothenburg, R Beare, London, S A Bergstrand, Gothenburg, Fr Berlingieri and G Berlingieri, Genova, W Birch Reynardson, London, Mrs Br Brilioth, Uppsala, L Buglass, New York, J Cantello, Montreal, S Cotton, London, Å Davidsson, Uppsala, K C Dollimore, London, L Delfs, Gothenburg, J Frøystein-Halvorsen, Oslo, N Gordon, London, J G R Griggs, London, P G Hasselrot, Stockholm, N Healy, New York, B R Hellberg, Gothenburg, O Hellberg, Gothenburg, N G Hudson, London, H Kačic, Dubrovnik, L Kihlberg, Gothenburg, E Kofoed, Copenhagen, P Latron, Paris, L Lindfelt, Gothenburg, P Lureau, Bordeaux, A Mathé, Buenos Aires, J Middelboe, Copenhagen, L Rahmn, Gothenburg, A Rein, Oslo, D Richter-Hannes, Rostock, Th Rinman, Gothenburg, H G Röhreke, Hamburg, A Schumacher, New York, H Stang-Lund, Kobe, L Strøm-Olsen, Oslo, J O Söderblom, Uppsala, H Voet, Antwerp, K Wijk-Broström, Glumslöv.

Some most valuable information has been put at my disposal by underwriters and others on the understanding that no names are mentioned. I thank these anonymous donors for their help and assistance.

Professor Grönfors did not abandon me after having suggested the subject for this study. I have greatly profited by his encouragement and interest, his suggestions and ideas throughout that long period when the signboard "Work in Progress" was up. I thank him for it all. Professor J Sandström has been patient, full of good advice and pertinent observations throughout. Professor Sj Braekhus kindly read an early version of the manuscript. His constructive criticism has been of great value for the final product. I have profited much from my visits to the Scandinavian Institute of Maritime Law in Oslo. The library is impressive, still more the helpfulness shown to me.

The distinguished lawyer Per Runeland, though no specialist in maritime law, gave me the benefit of his keen intellect in reading an early version of the manuscript. His insights and unbiased opinions were of great help to me and I wish to take this opportunity of thanking him.

My friend Lloyd Watkins, Secretary to the British Maritime Law Association, was kind enough to read the whole manuscript and with tact and discretion transformed many of my mistakes into readable English. Mrs M von Proschwitz MA gave me the same assistance in respect of the addenda introduced at a later stage. I thank them both for this valuable help.

Mrs I Ohlsson, particularly gifted in that she can cope with my handwriting, has typed the manuscript with talent and speed. My faithful secretaries Miss G Eklund and Mrs B Pamp have helped with the retyping, checking, copying and proof reading with their usual devotion to duty. The proper way to thank them is undoubtedly to promise them that there will be no more books.

Fonden för Sjörättslig Forskning has paid me the compliment of supporting this study financially for which I thank the trustees.

My obligation to my wife is immense for her constant help in listening to me and offering sound advice.

Finally I thank F V Voltaire for his warning: "*Le secret d'ennuyer est celui de tout dire*".[1] I have tried to pay attention to it.

Gothenburg, 9 October 1975   KAJ PINEUS

---

1.   Voltaire, *Satires du Mondain*, 1736.

Table of Cases and Abbreviations Used

AMC   American Maritime Cases
Asp. MLC   Aspinall's Maritime Law Cases
Fed.   Federal Reporter
Lloyd's Rep   Lloyd's Law Reports
Ll.L.Rep   Lloyd's List Law Reports
ND   Nordiske Domme i Sjøfartsanliggender
NJA   Nytt Juridiskt Arkiv
Swab Rep   Swabey's Reports
W. Rob.   William Robinson Reports
Hans OLG, JRPV   Hanseatische Oberlandesgericht sogleich Sammlung der
                        Rechtssprechung der Oberlandesgerichte Juristiche
                        Rundschau für Privat Versicherung

Page

A P Bernstorff, The *v. Lysaker II* S & H Rt. (1939) ND 260 17
Aberfoyle, The (1902) NJA 102; (1902) ND 121 107
Alkmeon Naviera *v. Marina L* (The) 1982 AMC 153 (9th Cir. 1980) 10
American Mail Line *v.* Skagit River Navigation & Trading Co, AMC 1375;
   91 F(2d) 835, 844–45 (9th Cir. 1937) 30
Amie, The (1973) ND 364 74

Blanche C Pendleton, The 1924 AMC 382, 384 (4th Cir. ED Va 1924) 8, 79, 102
Bytom, The (1955) NJA 386; (1955) ND 254 88

Cabin Cruiser, A (1979) ND 325 92
Castor, The (1932) 18 Asp. MLC 312; 43 Ll.L.Rep 261 .... 34, 40, 41, 95
Catamaran Miami Mae I, The 1969 AMC 216 (3rd Cir. 1963) 8
Clyde, The (1856) Swab. Rep 23. 8
Columbus, The (1849) 3 W. Rob. 158 18
Complaint of American Commercial Lines Inc. etc. 1973 AMC 319 (USC ED
   Kentucky) 113
Cranus, The (1956) ND 250 95
Cross Contracting Co *v.* Law 197 (AMC, US Ct. of App. 1008) 113

Dynafuel *v. Fernview*, The 1968 AMC 1996 (SDNY 1968) 10
Dyrstad, The (1960) ND 68 66

Edgar M Queeny, The *v. Corinthos*, The 1981 AMC 283 (ED Pa 1980) 15
Edison, The (1933) 18 Asp. MLC 380 .... 17, 40, 41
Elisabeth, The, Hans OLG Urt. v. 29.3 1935-Bf. I 334/35 JRPV 35.271 74
Ernest Pettus, The *v.* Jones and Laughlin Steel Corp. 1972 AMC 170 USDC (WD
   Penn) 112

Feiebas, The (1980) ND 78 93
Fire Island, The 1950 AMC 873 (5th Cir. 1950) 44

Gahr Development Inc. of Panama *v. Nedlloyd Marseilles*, The 1983 AMC 573
   USDC (ED La) 114
Geelong Harbour Trust Commissioners *v.* Gibbs Bright & Co (*The Octavian*)
   [1974] 1 Lloyd's Rep 344 99

Harmonides, The (1903) 9 Asp. MLC 334 .... 39, 41
Hazelmoor, The [1980] 2 Lloyd's Rep 351 16
Heddy, The (1935) NJA B No. 1049; (1935) ND 499 73
Hohenzollern, The (1906) 10 Asp. MLC 236 .... 39, 41
Huntington, The (tug) 1982 AMC 2588 (2nd Cir. 1982) 44

Ironmaster, The (1859) Swab. Rep 441 18

James L Hamilton, The 1973 AMC 319 USDC (ED Kentucky) 113

Kate, The (1899) 8 Asp. MLC 539 .... 18, 41
Kia Ora, The 252 Fed. 507 (4th Cir. 1918) 44
King Fisher Marine Service *v. N P Sunbound*, The 1984 AMC 1769 (5th Cir.
   1984) 12
Kong Alf, The (1945) ND 499 95
Kongedybet, The *v. Scanmail* S & H Rt. (1934) ND 325 17

La Salle, The 1973 AMC 319 USDC (ED Kentucky) 113
Lord Strathcona Steamship Co *v.* Dominion Coal Co (1925) 23 Ll.L.Rep. 145;
   [1926] A.C. 108 41
Leif, The *v. Eriksborg*, The (1955) NJA 119; (1955) ND 275 17
Lykaion, The, Il Diritto Marittimo 1972, p. 655 *et seq.* 42
Lyrma, (No. 1) The [1978] 2 Lloyd's Rep 27 .... 92, 108

Mannhem, The, HD 17 October 1898 (not in print) 107
Manningham, The (1897) NJA 596; (1900) NJA 2 .... 105, 108
Miles *v.* Rosenthal 1972 AMC 627 USDC (SDNY) 30

Namsos, The *v. Augusta*, The, Gulatings Lrt. (1938) ND 284 17
Neptune Lines *v.* Hudson Valley 1973 AMC 125 (SDNY 1972) 44
Norge, The (1900) NJA 2 106
Northumbria, The (1869) 3 A & E 6 18

Octavian, The [1974] 1 Lloyd's Rep 344 99
Olaf Scheel, The (1976) ND 389 93
Orange, The 1972 AMC 627 USDC (SDNY) 30, 58

Parkhaven, The (1920) ND 106 95
Philadelphia, The (1917) 14 Asp. MLC 68 18
Piper Aircraft Co *v. Geynold Reno*, The 1982 AMC 214 114
Premuda, The (1940) 67 Ll.L.Rep 9 44
President Madison, The 1937 AMC 1375 (9th Cir. 1937) 12
Prins Knud, The (1940) 67 Ll.L.Rep 458 44
Proteus, The *v.* Cushing 1925 AMC 779 (Sup. Ct.) 7, 18, 71

Queen Elizabeth, The (1949) 82 Ll.L.Rep 803 89

Rauha, The *v. Gunvall*, The (1934) NJA A.278; (1934) ND 284 17
Remoy, The (1982) ND 204 89
Rowan, The *v. Clan Malcolm*, The (1924) 18 Ll.L.Rep 394 69

Saint Anna, The [1980] 1 Lloyd's Rep 180 113
Saivo, The *v. Windward Island*, The (1959) ND 445 .... 17, 85
Sally, The (1979) ND 163 93
San Onofre, The (1917) 17 Asp. MLC 74 .... 35, 40, 95
Sea-Gull, The (1957) ND 579 65
Selma Thorden, The (Sup Ct, NJA 1951, p. 130) 13
Silia, The [1981] 2 Lloyd's Rep 534 113
Songa, The (1978) ND 164 92
Span Terza, The [1984] 1 Lloyd's Rep 119 113
Standard Oil Co of New Jersey *v.* Southern Pacific Co 268 US 146; 1925 AMC
   779, 782 102
Stigstad, The (1917) ND 81 38
Sunlong, The (1954) ND 664 95

Tercero, The (1955) ND 245 45
Tullikki, The (1975) ND 203; (1979) ND 111 .... 92, 108
Turret Age, The (1904) NJA 322 107

Umbria, The 166 US 404, 421 (1897) 80

Zanzibar Shipping *v.* Railroad locomotive engine No. 2199 1982 AMC 1420
   (SD Tex 1982) 10, 21

I

Introduction

Point of departure

As the Official Average Adjuster of Gothenburg for 44 years and ultimately for the whole of Sweden I signed 3,479 Statements and Adjustments. Few of them were in respect of cargo; most of them dealt with general average or hull insurance. I naturally became interested in the values of ships and could not fail to learn something about them. It therefore came as a surprise that when I addressed myself more closely to the subject of ship's value it proved so difficult to come to grips with it and to find simple and clear-cut answers to the many questions that arise in the course of my studies.

Value in the economic sense

When planning a study on ship's value one has first of all to consider what attention, if any, should be devoted to the concept of *value* in the sense it is used and explained in economic science and in philosophy. Should it contain as an introduction a survey of the *justum pretium* as explained by Thomas Aquinas? Should it then give a summary of the concept of value and wealth as indicated by Adam Smith in his *Wealth of Nations*? Should one from there go on to explain the nature and causes of wealth according to David Ricardo in his *Principles* of political economy and taxation? Having gone that far one would have to continue and take up *value* as it appears in the *Communist Manifesto* and the writing of Karl Marx, followed by a presentation of the theories of C Menger and W S Jevons, ending up with an overall picture of the concept of value held by the leaders in the field of economic science of today.

Already a perfunctory study of the 115 pages written by S Hagenauer[1] on the *justum pretium* was enough to make me realize that it would be highly doubtful if I would ever find my way out of this

---

1. Beiheft 24 zur *Vierteljahrschrift für Sozial- und Wirtschaftsgeschichte*, S Hagenauer: "Das 'justum pretium' bei Thomas von Aquino", Stuttgart 1931.

forest of theories as to the true meaning of value in a somewhat abstract sense. Assuming, however, that it would have been possible to reach the other side of that forest safely one would still have made little progress towards the ultimate destination, ship's value.

General observation on course and disposition followed

I have examined the prevalent ideas as to the true construction of value, not as explained in the economic science of today, but as indicated by modern legal authors when examining the value problems in connection with day-to-day life. Seen in that context the value concept becomes more easy to grasp and more useful for my investigations as to ship's value. It will come as no surprise that the legal theories on values depend very much on the purposes for which they are intended. To what extent, if any, can they be made usefully to apply to ship's value? This, it is hoped, will appear from this study.

The value of property appears in many shapes. To situate the problem of ship's value in the general context of what I term "models of value" an albeit brief survey is given of these various models as they appear in Scandinavian legal writing (Chapter 2). The analysis on how these models fit in with various aspects of ship's value that are dealt with in the following sections is done in connection with each particular problem taken up. This way of presenting the subject is, like any other system, open to criticism. It is bound in some places to lead to repetition and sometimes proceeding with an eye in the "driving mirror". It has nevertheless the advantage of making each section more self contained and it represents more truly the practitioner's approach to *ship's value*.

Ships' values are subject to fluctuations. It is therefore necessary to devote attention to the relevant time to apply when assessing ship's value for various purposes. The influence the time element may have on ship's value is explained in the section on market value in Chapter 2.

The English method of assessing ship's value is somewhat different from the method used elsewhere. Much attention will necessarily have to be devoted to it in a study of this kind. The method is explained in Chapter 6 which deals with the influence of the charterparty. The effects of it are shown in those particular sections where its impact is felt. This will make the problem appear in several places and may therefore not satisfy those who in a study of this kind prefer the

Versailles type of garden to the English park but it does undoubtedly serve to illustrate how the English method works out in practice.

Itinerary

The first six chapters I devote to general issues relating to ship's value. What do we mean by value? Is it the *market value*, the *dividend value*, the *expectation value*, the *utility value*? Or is it the *replacement value* or the *liquidation value*? What do these definitions actually mean? These aspects are dealt with in Chapter 2. In Chapter 3 I take up the time element, giving as an introduction some striking examples of the fluctuations of ship's values in comparatively short periods. The exact date of ship's value is important for collision, general average, salvage and under some limitation systems; the value over a period of time is relevant for credit purposes and for hull insurance.

Ship's valuers, from what profession they come and how they are appointed is illustrated in Chapter 4. The elements the ship valuers take into account in assessing ship's value are dealt with in Chapter 5 as well as the impact of the rise in bunker oil prices between the 1st and 2nd editions of this book. In Chapter 6 I take up the charterparty and the influence it is allowed to have in assessing ship's value in England.

Having dealt with the general issues I approach the particular instances where ship's value is of importance.

The problems of evaluating ship's value for credit purposes are dealt with in Chapter 7. The approach to ship's value for hull insurance I discuss in Chapter 8. Assessing ship's value in collision and salvage cases is dealt with in Chapters 9 and 10. They also contain a further evaluation of the English method of valuation as explained in Chapter 6.

General average and ship's value are discussed in Chapter 11. I deal in Chapter 12 with limited liability, I explain the *fortune de mer* system and make a comparison with the working of the 1976 Convention on Limitation of Liability by using as an example the effect for the vessel *Eve*, ending the chapter with a brief evaluation of the two systems.

I conclude the study with a Summary and the conclusions drawn from the preceding chapters.

Law and legal sources

It will be necessary in order to get a proper view of the problems at hand to look abroad and not confine the study to Swedish or Scandinavian law. The risk of mistakes and misunderstanding multiply thereby. Even when well founded, such criticism as I shall feel free to express may not be welcome everywhere.[2] It is nevertheless necessary to run this risk in order to illustrate some aspects of the problem dealt with.

The maritime lawyer has an advantage over his colleagues in other fields of law. By and large maritime law is similar on many essential points the world over. This simplifies the author's task. If he gets to grips with Scandinavian and English law without therefore excluding Continental law he has probably secured an overall picture of the subject. There are no doubt gaps. Spanish legal writing and court decisions in the Spanish language have had to be left out for linguistic reasons. The same is true for Japan, except that some information on practice will appear in some places. Only glimpses of the law and decisions of the Soviet Union appear. Thus the study does not cover the subject taking into account the maritime law of the whole world. Whether in spite of these limitations it will present a sufficiently broad view of the subject is for the reader to judge.

Need of a study of this kind

When starting out on this study about ship's value and during my labours with it I have many times thought of the words in *Ecclesiastes*: "of making many books there is no end; and much study is a weariness of the flesh".[3] Not because I wanted to shrink from my self-imposed task but because I asked myself: "Is this book necessary? The practical world knows how to buy and sell ships, how to use vessels as securities for loans, how to arrive at salvage remunerations, how to assess the proper collision recovery, how to draw up general average statements and there indicate ship's contributing value. Will those engaged in practical affairs have to look into a book to do it all? And if so would they look into this one? Why then this wearisome study?"

I pick up the gauntlet thrown by Ben Sirach. I submit it is

---

2. *Cf.* in this connection what was said by the Swedish Archbishop N Söderblom at the Gaudy in Oxford 1923 on being made a Doctor of Civil Law: "I know of no other modern equivalent rendering of the ancient Greek word *barbaros* than the English *foreigner*".

3. *Ecclesiastes* nr. 12: 12 in the Chapter "Advice to a young man". The author of *Ecclesiastes* was Ben Sirach and the time of publication about 180 BC.

worthwhile to clarify problems, to get to know what one is doing and why, to illustrate as fully as possible the problems involved. If this can eventually help to bring about international uniformity in practice where there is none at present, so much the better.

2

Values in General

Introduction

Much has been written, in Sweden and elsewhere, about the subject of value. This is hardly surprising. Property is sold and purchased. Property is lost and its value recovered from the underwriters. Property is destroyed and a claim for damages made against the tortfeasor. Property is used as a collateral for loans and its value assessed for that purpose. Property is expropriated and a claim made against the public authorities. Property appears as an asset in the books of a company; what is the highest value of it that is acceptable under the company law in force and by the auditors? What is the lowest value permissible under applicable tax law? What is the value of the property from which to calculate the permissible depreciation? With what value shall the property figure in an estate that is subject to death duties or gift tax? If a sale or purchase tax applies on what value of the property should it apply? What does the value "declared for Customs purposes" actually represent?

In all these cases the value of the property has to be ascertained. What guidelines, methods or models should be followed?

Demarcation lines

This study will not deal with ship's value for tax purposes. National tax legislation is a province of its own that varies from one country to the other. Its application to ship's value seen in an international context is well worth a study of its own, which should however be consigned to the expert on tax law.

The way ship's value appears in the company's book is the result of a complex interplay of tax regulations, provisions in the applicable company law, the financial result for the individual ship or the whole fleet of the company, as the case may be, the depreciation scheme adopted by the company or generally followed where the shipowner has his activities. These problems, highly interesting as they are, cannot properly be pressed into a study of this kind however.

Ship's value obviously plays an important role when a shipping partnership is dissolved, a single ship company is wound up or when there is a change of partnership or share owner. The price to be put on the ship in transactions of this kind will depend on its market value at the relevant time—whatever that time is if the parties do not agree to this—but the partner or shareholder will want a proportion of the other assets of the partnership or company as well. The price a partner or a shareholder will obtain will also depend on the influence the proportion of the partnership or the number of shares have in the running of the ship.[1] To all this comes the incidence of applicable tax provisions. Investigations made go to show that the value of the ship as such is not easy to make out separately from the many factors that have a bearing on the price obtained for the respective partnership or shares.

I submit that what has been said should suffice to explain why I hold the view that ship's value in the context of tax legislation, company law and the sale of shares or the winding up of a shipowning company has a purpose of its own and does not have its proper place in a study devoted to ship's value.

Market value

The natural point of departure for a discussion on the value of property is the *market value*. This has variously been defined as the highest price the ordinary seller may obtain when selling his property, respectively the lowest price the ordinary purchaser will pay for it.[2]

The US Supreme Court said that the market value in respect of ships was "established by contemporaneous sales of like property in the way of ordinary business, as in the case of merchandise sold in the market".[3] A succinct definition is no doubt this one: "The worth of

1. *Cf. Expulsion or Oppression of Business Associates* "Squeeze Outs in Small Enterprises" prepared by Duke University NC 1961 (F Hodge O'Neal and J Derwin) where it is said *inter alia*. "The difficulty in properly establishing the value of an interest in a close corporation or other small business lies in the complexity and subjective nature of any valuation process. Each valuation is unique." It then goes on to quote a passage from I Dewing: *The Financial Policy of Corporations*, p. 285 (4th edn., 1941) where it is said: "Value is subjective; it is based on individual experience. Hence, when the individual tries to find an objective standard or criterion for his own personal values, he is confronted with endless confusion . . . In the end the test of value is pragmatic— where does the judgment of most men meet? It is the composite of many judgments, not the reaching for an illusory fixed and varying basis of value on which judgment of all men should agree".

2. C Welander, p. 51. C Ljungholm, p. 144, *et seq.*

3. *Proteus* v. *Cushing*, 1925 AMC 779 (Sup Ct).

the thing is the price it will bring".[4] Thus unless there is a prospective buyer the market will not function.[5] The seller of the property, for example, a large house intended for private use, may discover that there is no market value for it.[6]

As against this concrete approach to the problem of value *cf.* Danielsson, at p. 14, who says (my translation): "There is a widespread view about economic value as an actual character of things, performances and rights the existence of which can be ascertained and with a degree of objectivity". This sounds somewhat incomprehensible in English and I put down the Swedish text as well "Det finnes en mycket spridd uppfatt ning om ekonomiskt värde som en faktisk egenskap hos saker, presentationer och rättigheter, vilkens förhandenvaro och grad av objektivitet kan konstateras". This, as I understand it, is somehow to say that to many the economic value of a thing is not what it will fetch if sold, the value is rather an objective entity pertaining to the goods itself.

Assuming, however, that the property is attractive as such it must be underlined that the basic concept of the market value is a climate where the prospective seller and purchaser are free to come to terms. Where public authorities restrict the sale and purchase of the particular property by import or export regulations, by maximum prices or quota provisions, the market value concept has little meaning, if any. This is even more so in those countries that apply the state economy where the market value does not form part of the accepted philosophy.

What then constitutes the market value in a free or mixed economy? For commodities like coffee, copper, etc., that are regularly quoted on the commodity exchange the market value will be such quotations at the relevant time. An actual shipment may have been invoiced at a different price owing to the date of the contract or because of other special circumstances. It is safe to say though that the "market value" of such a shipment is nevertheless the general quotation of the commodity at the relevant time.

For the goods brought home from the supermarket for daily

---

4. The *Blanche C Pendleton* 1924 AMC, pp. 382, 384 (4th Cir. 1924). The words also appear in the English case *The Clyde* (1856). See Roscoe, at p. 31 cited from Swabey's Reports, 1855–59, at p. 23.

5. The *Catamaran Miami Mae I* 1969 AMC 216 (3rd Cir. 1963).

6. That type of property is sometimes described as a "white elephant" which illustrates the point. *Cf.* J Attali, *Un homme d'influénce*, Paris, 1985, p. 121. The rhinoceros of the Hagenbeck Zoo pledged to Max Warburg as security for a loan of DM 8,000 to buy *food*; the animal was later sold to the Budapest Zoo.

consumption the market price will be the amount paid at the cash desk. Taking as a third example, the new car, the market price is the price officially announced by the producer. The discount that in some cases may be obtained from the dealer should not qualify this assertion unless common enough to make the "official price" only a nominal one. There are, however, a number of goods that cannot be made to fit into any of the types just mentioned. What about the prices obtained for yearlings at the annual auctions of racehorses in one of the centres of that trade, or of antiquities and art treasures sold by a well-known auctioneer in the great cities of the world? Do the prices obtained indicate the market value of such highly individual objects as a young would-be racehorse or a set of genuine Chippendale chairs? Perhaps we are now approaching a more general answer to the question of what constitutes the market price.

A path is where many people have walked the same way. Likewise, the market value is where many people have paid more or less the same price for the property sold and purchased. The hiker in the mountains does not always have a path he can follow. He may have to look for the next cairn to be sure he is taking the right direction. Likewise, when there are not enough deals made for a path to be easily discernible the parties will have to look for the cairns, that is to say any relevant deals made in or about the period under consideration.[7]

The above does not purport to be a clear-cut definition of what constitutes the market value in all circumstances; and this because I cannot make myself believe that there is any all-embracing formula that can be made to apply in all cases. Let me try my hand at a paradox, like all such something of a half truth. The market value is the meeting point of two different concepts, one of which must necessarily be erroneous, i.e. the seller's belief that the price will fall and the buyer's confidence in a rising market.

Dividend value

When the seller and the purchaser do agree on the price and this price can be understood to mean the market value of the property, what considerations did they have in mind? Did they attach importance to what is sometimes termed the *dividend value*?[8] This is, perhaps, a too literal translation of the Swedish term *avkastningsvärde*, that is to say

7. *Cf.* I Dewing: *The Financial Policy of Corporations* quoted above.
8. Flodhammar, p. 102, *et seq*; Hernmark, p. 111; Persson, Studier, p. 6; Braekhus, p. 38

the value arrived at when taking into account the earnings of the subject-matter, present and future. One might explain it as the *present discounted value*[9] of the future stream of income derived from the property; or to put it in other words, the difference between the present value on the one hand of future gross income and future expenditure on the other. "Dividend value" has the advantage of being brief and bearing in mind the explanation given here I feel entitled to use it here and elsewhere.

Assessing future earnings properly will depend on the lifetime ascribed to the property, or at any rate to the period of time the purchaser intends to use it, the earnings that ensue from existing long-term contracts and whether these contain an index clause or not. If there are no contracts it is the knowledge of earnings of other similar property and the flair, if any, of the prospective purchaser that will guide him. The future expenditure may consist of interest on contracted loans, cost of upkeep and cost of manpower necessary for the continued use of the property. While the rate of interest may sometimes be fixed for a comparatively long period the other two items will in most cases show an upward trend. How steeply the curve will rise will depend on many circumstances, mostly beyond the control of the seller and the purchaser.

Expectation value

We have met this concept already when referring to the prices paid for yearlings at racehorse auctions. It applies also for ships, e.g. a vessel of specialized design built by a shipyard for a potential customer in the hope it will prove suitable for a certain type of trade.

Replacement value

Another method of assessing the value of the property is to use its *replacement value*[10] defined as the cost of new similar property after

9. ". . . the discounted future earning power of a ship . . . and as such a factor to be used in determining market value" the court said in *Alkmeon Naviere* v. *Marina L*, 1982 AMC 153 (9th Cir. 1980).

10. Some US courts have refused to allow replacement cost to be used if the vessel was obsolete on the ground that it is unreasonable to consider that anybody would want to replace the vessel. See, for instance, *Dynafuel* v. *Fernview*, 1968 AMC 1966 (SDNY 1968); *Zanzibar Shipping* v. *Railroad locomotive engine* No. 2199, 1982 AMC 1420 (SD Tex. 1982). Hellner: *Försäkringsrätt*, p. 226 *et seq.*; Grundt, p. 210 *et seq.*; Persson: *Skada och värde*, p. 305 *et seq.* and Studier, p. 5. Rodière-Lureau No. 57.

deduction for wear and tear. In order to use that method properly it is necessary to know the answer to a number of questions. Is the property of a standardized type, where the cost of similar property can easily be ascertained? Then the cost of a new object should normally cause few problems. This is not necessarily so always. The price of a property of foreign origin may have gone up because of a change in the rate of exchange. The standardized property, say a semi-detached house, may take time to replace. The time factor will make it more difficult to indicate costs of replacement. An index clause in the replacement contract may influence the ultimate cost of "new similar property". In those cases where the property is not of more or less standardized type the replacement value method will hardly work in a satisfactory way. As with the replacement cost the meaning to be ascribed to deductions for wear and tear will depend on a number of factors:[11] what type of property it is, what "life expectancy" it has and how much of it has elapsed, whether the property has been used roughly or not, what amount has been invested in its upkeep to counteract the effect of age and use. Thus in the highly competitive liner trade, where the ships must be technically up to date, the depreciation rate will necessarily have to be much higher than for the ordinary tramp vessel.

Rather than go into the finer shades of these elements the parties may resort to some standardized depreciation based on age, running hours or follow the depreciation plan adopted by the trade for that particular type of property or take guidance from the depreciation percentage permissible under the relevant tax laws, although in my view these should only be made to serve as an indication rather than as conclusive evidence as to the proper replacement value.

Inflation may increase the cost of replacement, whereas an economic depression may reduce the value of the object to be replaced far below what follows from ordinary wear and tear principles. The proper application of the replacement value rule will sometimes cause difficult problems.

11. The deduction, Rodhe says (p. 216) shall not be that large that one arrives at the selling price; one might then as well have taken that value directly rather than making the detour over the replacement values less depreciation, which had better be of a linear nature say five years and 20% p.a. which would mean that in case the loss occurs after two years a 40% deduction should be made as already written off from the original value.

Utility value

When agreeing on the price did the parties take into account the *utility value*[12] of the property, that is to say the usefulness of it in the hands of the seller or of the purchaser , i.e. her value as a going concern.[13] This is akin to the dividend value discussed above except that accent is placed on the extra value the property may have because it is particularly well suited to the trade in which one of the parties engaged, e.g. because of her construction.[14] The contracts entered into or about to be entered into for the use of the property are perhaps more favourable than follows from the overall situation in the market; in this sense the utility value would add to the value of the property. The concept of the utility values as will be shown in the section on value for credit purposes is closely connected with what values the favourable contracts referred to have in the hands of a new owner.

Liquidation value

When assessing the value of a company one method resorted to is to find out its *liquidation value* or to use the Swedish term its *slaughter value*,[15] that is to say the difference between the assets and the liabilities of the company. The method is not confined to those cases where the company has been wound up. In practice it will produce a low figure compared with the other methods indicated above. For the purpose of this study the liquidation value method is, I should say, confined to the forced sale of the vessel. From the proceeds obtained at the public auction, where incidentally a minimum price is fixed by those creditors entitled to a share in it, the balance between the minimum price (or the actual price obtained if above that price) and the claims of those creditors who are entitled to a share in the proceeds will constitute the *liquidation value* of the vessel.

This enumeration of different types of value or rather methods or models on how to arrive at the value of a property show that the term "value" is not an exact or precise term.[16] The price obtained for a

12. Tiberg, *Kreditsäkerheten*, p. 99 *et seq.*, Riska, p. 100; Grönfors, *Ägande och Brukande*, p. 9.

13. The courts in the USA will resort to this rule only where the vessel is of a peculiar or unique construction or of a special use to the owner. The *President Madison* (1937) AMC 1375 (9th Cir. 1937). *King Fisher Marine Service* v. *N P Sunbound* 1984 AMC 1769 (5th Cir. 1984).

14. For example, a vessel of Panmax type or one reinforced for winter traffic in the Baltic or, to be quite specific, a vessel constructed to carry limestone from the Island of Gotland (site of the City of Visby) to the cement works on the mainland.

15. Flodhammer, *op. cit.*, and also Hellner, *op. cit.*

16. Selvig, p. 21 *et seq.* also p. 51 *et seq.*

property when sold in a free market is different from the one obtained when price regulations are in force.[17] The price the owner of a property will be adjudged in an expropriation suit will depend on many factors clearly indicated in the law but not least whether the average local price for real estate is already established in the region or not.[18] The value for credit purposes is rarely the same as the purchase price.[19] Nor is the amount claimed from a tortfeasor necessarily the same as the market value.[20]

Value in respect of ships

Something can be found in the literature on the general approach as to values in respect of ships.[21] Discussing whether to introduce in Swedish law the registration of charterparties and using them as collateral for loans, the Swedish Maritime Law Committee mentioned (SOU 1970: 74, p. 136 *et seq.*) that ship's value could be assessed in different ways. For mortgage purposes the price that could be obtained at a sale of the vessel obviously came into the foreground. That price had a natural link with the market value. Another value was the cost of building or the price for which the vessel was bought. Terms like dividend value and utility value, the Committee said, are also used where ship's earnings under certain conditions will obviously materially affect ship's sale value and her market value. The Committee did not decide, and had no mission to do so, which, if any, of the values were the correct ones to be used. Some words about ships' values are to be found in Ritter, p. 855, where he enumerates *"Gebrauchswert, Ertragswert, Verkaufswert, Anschau-*

---

17. Hellner, *op. cit.*, p. 232; Jørgensen, Lyngsø, Tranow I, p. 146 *et seq.*
18. Hernmark, *op. cit.*, p. 106 *et seq.*
19. See section below on ship's value for credit purposes.
20. Grönfors, *Trafikskadeansvar*, p. 39 *et seq.*; Karlgren, p. 142 *et seq. Cf.* in this connection Rodhe (p. 217) who says that the use of the selling value of the property as the basis for a claim for damages for a loss is a somewhat uncertain method. That transaction has in fact not taken place. To be on the safe side one had better reduce the would-be selling value by way of using the purchase value. Assuming the property was bought with the intention of resale the purchase price appears as more reliable and trustworthy than the higher value that may be indicated by the market situation. Article 120 of the Swedish Maritime Code does not say what value should be used for assessing damages. The Supreme Court in *The Selma Thordén* (NJA 1951 p. 130) used the selling value whereas the courts below had used the purchase price to which they added freight, additional charges, costs of discharge and forwarding.
21. Seven methods of establishing ship's value in connection with salvage are indicated by one or rather two authors (see p. 44, fn. 23). They will be explained in the chapter devoted to Salvage (Chapter 10).

affungswert, Herstellungswert". Which of these values should be used for insurance purposes will depend, he says, *"aus dem Wesen des Eigentümerinteresse"*.

In the following sections I will look into ship's value for different purposes. I shall examine there if, and if so to what extent, the theories,[22] models and methods of valuation indicated above can be made to apply to the particular aspects dealt with.

22. As for legal theories in general the following passage from M Matesco, *Le Droit Maritime Sovietique face au Droit Occidental*, Paris 1966, p. 58 *et seq.* is interesting: "Faisant sienne, sans réserves, la critique apportée au dogmatisme juridique lors du XX Congrès du P.C.U.S le revue 'L'Etat et le droit sovietique a publié un éditorial bien connu' (No. 2 1956) intitulé Le XX Congrès du P.C.U.S. et les tâches de la science juridique sovietique . . . Mais, poursuivit l'éditorial, tout cela s'est passé à une époque à laquelle la grande propagation du culte de la personalité* a eu un role négatif dans le développement de la science juridique sovietique; époque dans laquelle au lieu de généraliser, profondément, les pratiques résultant de l'édification de l'Etat et du droit socialiste et, sur cette base, de les étudier, d'une manière créatrice, les juristes sovietiques ont glissé sur la pente de la citomanie, en répétant, de manière livresque, des vérités généralement connues . . . et ont eu peur de formuler, avec courage, des thèmes nouvelles, conformes au développements de la vie.

"C'est pourquoi de développement futur de la science juridique *droit être intégralement subordonné aux besoin de la pratique*, nécessaire à la construction du communism . . . La liaison entre le théorie et la pratique doit être directe et multilatérale *pour toutes les branches de la science juridique*".

* in the notes explained as: "Culte de Stalin".

Cf. in connection with this note: "A normally built truth lives—I should say—as a rule 17 to 18 up to 20 years seldom more" (H Ibsen: *An Enemy of the People*, 1882, Act IV).

3

The Time Element

Introduction

Even a perfunctory knowledge of ships' prices makes you familiar with the rapid rise and fall of ships' values. Numerous examples could be cited to illustrate the point. Let me give a few.

A bulk carrier of 65,000 tons deadweight, and two years old, was worth US$23 million in July 1974 and $18 million at the end of the year (a loss of 21.7% in six months). A vessel of 52,000 tons, built in 1965, was sold in February 1974 for $13.5 million whereas a similar vessel one year older was sold for $7.6 million in November 1974 (a loss of 44% in nine months). The trend may be an upward one as well. A shelterdeck vessel of 12,000 tons and 15 years old was worth $2.5 million in January 1974 and $3.4 million at the end of the year (a gain of 36% in 11 months). A small 3,100-ton tanker was sold for Swedish kronor 7.1 million in June 1974 and for 8.9 million kronor two months later (a gain of 25%).

To these examples from the First Edition of this book (1975) I will add some more recent ones. A bulk carrier of 65,000 tons dw five years old was worth US$21 million in January 1981 and $6 million in January 1983 (a depreciation of 74% in two years). An eight-year-old turbine tanker of 25,000 tons was worth $20 million in January 1980 and $3.5 million in December 1982 (a loss of 82.5% in not quite three years).[1]

These examples will suffice to show that ship's values are subject to considerable fluctuations, the relevant periods being sometimes months not years.[2] In the circumstances it is essential for a study devoted to ship's value to indicate what is the relevant time that counts when assessing ship's value for different purposes.

As a result of a collision on 31 January 1975 with the *Edgar M*

1. I have selected these examples from the vast amount of material kindly put at my disposal by B Hellberg and L Kihlberg, shipbrokers of my home port Gothenburg, by T Rinman of *The Swedish Shipping Gazette* and by Mr R C Sculpher of Casebourne, Leach & Co, London.

2. The *Edgar M Queeny* v. *Corinthos* 1981 AMC 283 (ED Pa 1980).

15

Queeny, the *Corinthos* was sunk. Those interested in the *Corinthos* claimed for the loss on the basis of the price obtained at the sale of a similar vessel in November 1974. A witness called by the *Edgar M Queeny* testified that "the tanker market in late January 1975 was disastrous and had dropped tremendously". The court preferred the value obtained at the sale of a similar vessel on 31 January 1975, the day of the collision, as being more reliable, the market for the types of ships involved having dropped so dramatically in the preceding two months (*cf.* p. 30).

See also [1980] 2 Lloyd's Rep 351: *The Hazelmoor*. The buyer defaulted on the sale's contract. The vessel was sold four months after the contract date. The seller claimed damages, i.e. loss of 54.5% on the contract price.

Hull insurance

Ship's value for insurance purposes may be its value at the inception of the risk[3] or the value at any given time while the insurance is in force,[4] that is to say at the time of the loss. Which one applies will depend on the provisions in national law and the insurance conditions. Where ship's value is a sum agreed upon by the parties this value will represent ship's value at the inception of the risk and will in principle not be influenced by the time element. Where a ship is insured "up to an amount of . . ." (i.e. an open policy) her true value becomes relevant when the ship is lost and a claim for total loss is made under the policy. This means that the different outlook as to the relevant time as explained is no longer maintained. The effect of an increase or fall in ship's value during the insurance period and the influence, if any, this may have on the settlement to be made will be examined in the section dealing with hull insurance (Chapter 8).

Value for credit purposes

When a creditor grants a loan using the ship as collateral, the value of the ship at the time the credit is granted will obviously be the time to be taken into account, but the creditor will watch out to make sure that during the whole credit period ship's value represents adequate security. He may have taken care of that risk at the inception of the risk by assessing a low value of the ship or granting credit that gives

3. The situation in, e.g. Denmark, England and Norway.
4. This applies to Sweden, *cf,* below, in the section on hull insurance (Chapter 8).

him an adequate safety margin, or both. If this is so, it is correct to say for credit purposes that ship's value at the inception of the credit risk is relevant and its value during the whole period of the credit will be watched closely.

Collision recovery

When a ship is lost owing to a collision the owner is entitled to recover from the tortfeasor the value of his ship. When fixing the date on which that value should be assesed the answer from the practitioners sometimes gets confused. It is pointed out that the generally accepted theory about *restitutio in integrum* means that the shipowner is entitled to recover the value of the vessel lost and also to receive compensation for the time it will take him to obtain another ship, the replacement costs, the loss to him because the vessel was particularly well suited for the service on which it was employed, the loss of freight based on the general freight market or the contract of affreightment entered into. All these elements go into the claim that is made and the time element for assessing the value of the vessel lost can hardly for practical purposes be properly disentangled from these other elements that constitute the true measure of damages. I can understand this pragmatic approach to the problem. Nevertheless, it should not prove too difficult to fix the proper time that should be used for assessing ship's value in a collision case, and it has so far as I am aware not caused too many problems. Scandinavian legal writers have not committed themselves on this particular point. Parallels can no doubt be drawn from Art. 37 of the Swedish Insurance Act where it is said that the claim against underwriters shall be the replacement cost less depreciation "immediately before the accident". The Scandinavian courts would appear to use the date of the collision as the relevant date or period for assessment of ship's value in connection with collision recovery.[5] The value of the ship as a going concern is at the time and place of the loss, the House of Lords said.[6] The value at the time of the loss is the view expressed in Belgium[7] and

---

5. *Cf. Rauha* v. *Gunwall* Sw. Sup. Ct. NJA 1934 A. 278 ND 1934, p. 284; *Kongedybet* v. *Scanmail* S. & H.Rt ND 1934, p. 325; *Namsos* v. *Augusta* Gulatings Lrt ND 1938, p. 284; *A P Bernstorff* v. *Lysaker II* S. & H.Rt. ND 1939, p. 260; *Leif* v. *Eriksborg* Sw. Sup. Ct. NJA 1955, p. 119; ND 1955, p. 275 *et seq. Saivo* v. *Windward Island* St. Ct. ND 1959, p. 445.

6. *The Edison* (1933) 18 Asp MLC, p. 380 *et seq.* See also Digest 5 Lloyd's Rep p. 217.

7. C Smeesters and G Winkelmolen, *Droit Maritime et Droit Fluvial*, Vol. III, Brussels 1938, p. 326.

also in France.[8] Rodière and Lureau[9] submit, however, that the value on the day that judgment is given, not the value at the time of the collision, should be decisive for the compensation. The market value at the time of the destruction of the vessel is the relevant time, the US Supreme Court has said.[10,11]

The complications that may sometimes arise in calculating the recovery in respect of loss of freight and profit should not make one deviate from the fundamental and, to me, correct principle that the date of the collision is the time to be used in assessing ship's value in the action against a third party.

8. J P Govare and J Warot, "La Fixation des dommages intérets en matière d'abordage en droit français," in *Studi in Onore di Giorgio Berlingieri*, Genova 1964, p. 216.

9. Rodière and Lureau No. 53 and No. 57. They indicate in support of their view that ship's value may have risen from 10,000 to 15,000 between the collision and the date of judgment.

But what about a fall in ship's value in that period? And what about the upward or downward trend in ships' prices between the judgment of the first court and the court of appeal to which the case may be brought? I cannot make myself accept as correct an assessment of time that allows developments that happen after the event that gave rise to the claim for collision damages to influence the quantum damage in respect of ship's value.

10. 1925 AMC p. 779 (Sup Ct.) *Proteus* v. *Cushing*.

11. *Revue de Droit Maritime Comparé*, Vol. 12, Paris 1925, p. 149 *et seq.* commenting *inter alia* on the time aspect in *Proteus* v. *Cushing* decision says:

"Arrivons maintenant à la date à laquelle il faut se placer pour estimer la valeur de navire coulé. En principe, ce doit être la date du jour de la perte; en ce sens, *Mittelstein*, Das Recht der Binnenschiffahrt dans *Ehrenberg*, Handbuch des gesamten Handelsrechts, 376; et pour la jurisprudence anglaise, *The Clyde*, précité; *The Ironmaster*, *The Columbus* et *The Philadelphia*, précités.

"Toutefois, il peut y avoir des cas où, en apparence, il en est autrement. Supposons, en effet, que le navire coulé était affrété. Son propriétaire est en droit, nous allons le voir, de réclamer le fret qu'il aurait gagné. Mais ce fret ne peut être que le fret net. En particulier, il y aura lieu de déduire du fret brut une certaine somme correspondant au pourcentage de la dépréciation qu'aurait subie le navire pendant la durée de la charte-partie. Or il a été jugé, en Angleterre, que, pour fair ressortir cette dépréciation, il y avait lieu d'estimer la valeur que le navire aurait eue à la fin de la chartepartie, *The Kate* (1899) p. 165; *The Racine* (1906) p. 273; rappr., *The Northumbria* (1869) 3 A & E 6. Cela revient, en effet, au même que de calculer la valeur du navire à la date de la collision et d'évaluer séparément le pourcentage de dépréciation pendant la durée de la charte-partie afin de le déduire du fret brut qui a été perdu. Mais il faut bien comprendre que cette évaluation du navire à la date d'expiration de la charte-partie ne peut se recommander qu'à titre de procédé empirique afin de faire ressortir le pourcentage de dépréciation dont nous venons de parler. Il ne faudrait pas en conclure qu'au cas d'élévation du marché entre le jour de la collision et celui de l'expiration de la charte-partie, la victime de l'arbordage serait en droit de réclamer une allocation correspondant à cette élévation de prix en plus de son fret net, *The Philadelphia*, précité. Ce résultat serait certainement inexact. Tout au plus pourrait-on admettre que l'élévation des prix du marché annulerait le pourcentage de dépréciation ou cas où elle lui serait supérieure ou équivalente, *The Philadelphia*, précité."

Salvage and general average

The salvors undertake to bring the ship and her cargo to a place of safety. The salvage services come to an end there and that will also indicate that this constitutes the relevant time for calculating ship's value for salvage purposes. For general average the assessment of ship's value should be based on its value at the termination of the adventure. There is a discrepancy between these two dates, the practical consequences of which will be looked into in the section on general average (Chapter 11).

Limitation of liability

Where limitation of shipowner's liability is based on the *fortune de mer* system as in the USA and in a number of other countries[12] the relevant time for assessing ship's value is the end of the voyage.

Other aspects on ship's value

I explained under the heading "Values in general" (Chapter 2) why I do not take up in the study ship's value in connection with (i) tax law, (ii) company law and (iii) shipping partnership. There are many complicated problems involved. I draw attention to some of them. When a shipping partnership is dissolved what is the relevant time for assessing ship's value? Assuming the partners do not agree is the time the vessel is sold the correct date? Or is it ship's value when steps were initiated to dissolve the partnership that counts? What about the rise or fall in tonnage values between those dates? All these elements are important for arriving at the proper value to be taken into account. They are involved and complicated and deserve the full attention of some other legal writer.

12. The states where the ship's value is used in some form or another for limitation purposes are indicated in Chapter 12.

4

Assessment of Ship's Value:
the Practical Approach

Who is to give the would-be purchaser of a ship the expert advice as to the price to pay? Who will give the salvors, the average adjuster, the court or the credit institutions the advice they may need for assessing ship's value? By and large the answer is, the shipbrokers. They are professionally engaged in arranging the sale and purchase of ships. To that end they will make available to themselves through their colleagues in other countries lists of vessels that are up for sale and of vessels that have actually been sold indicating the price obtained. Some shipbrokers concentrate on the home market, some on small or specialized ships. Their advice and services will be sought in cases where their specialist knowledge is material.

The shipbrokers will more often than not be able to assess ship's value either by bringing about the actual purchase or sale himself or by making comparisons with other deals with which they are professionally familiar.

When an official valuation certificate is needed by the court, by the average adjuster or by the salvors, etc., the way such a document is to be obtained forms part of the administrative law of each country. The experts may be appointed by the court. They may be asked to appear in court to give evidence as to how and why they have assessed ship's value in the way indicated. Their written opinion may be submitted to the court and may be accepted and become the court's own decision in the matter which is open to appeal like other court decisions. Or the experts may be picked from an official list prepared by the authorities and give their expert opinion according to official regulations that apply for their activities as expert valuers and/or ship's surveyors.

The assessment made by a well qualified broker, sometimes assisted by a naval architect, will in most cases be accepted by salvors, adjusters, arbitrators and/or the courts. When different sets of experts reach different conclusions the situation becomes more complicated.[1,2]

In another connection[3] I wrote as follows: The value given by experts (ship's valuers, assessors, shipbrokers, surveyors, naval architects) may sometimes strike the adjuster as remarkably high or low, compared with the agreed value of the insurance policy. He will probably obtain another valuation from a different expert, compare the two and if the discrepancies are small use the arithmetical mean.

1. *Cf.* AIDE Cambridge, p. 64. In most countries the expert valuers have no official status. Mostly shipbrokers, surveyors or naval architects are used or a combination of them. In some places they may have a slightly more official character in that they have an authorization from a Chamber of Foreign Trade, appear on a list of experts established by a Public Authority or, in case of dispute, are appointed by the tribunal.

The value of the ship which is accepted by the arbitrators in a salvage case will in most cases be accepted as evidence by the adjuster for general average purposes.

2. In the case *Zanzibar Shipping* v. *Railroad locomotive engine* No. 2199, 1982 AMC 1420 (SD Tex 1982) two experts gave opinions as to the value of the lost vessel in a collision, one for $21,000 and one for $35 million! The court commented on the two opinions: "This is not a shadowland, but the twilight zone" (Ibid., p. 1425).

3. K Pineus, *General Average. The practical problems*, p. 29, Gothenburg 1965.

5

Market Value

Introduction

The way a valuation certificate is formulated is not standardized nor does it follow any pattern officially or unofficially laid down. I use the following examples merely to get a solid platform from which to start my analysis of the various elements that go into making the market value of a ship.

Certificate of valuation

I give one example of a valuation certificate in order to illustrate the relevant points:

This is to certify that the undersigned . . . . . . has by request of . . . . . . valued the ro/ro vessel . . . . . . described as follows . . . . . .
about . . . . tons deadweight
Built in . . . . . . by . . . . . . Loaded draught . . . . . . GRT . . . . . .
NRT . . . . . .
Survey   /   19
Cont. Cap. . . . . . . TEU . . . . . .
Trailer lane length . . . . . .Rectangular cubic . . . . . . cbft
Stern door/ramp
Main engine
Speed about . . . . knots
Bow propeller
Dimensions

Then comes the concluding formula which may read:

Having regarded ship's age, size, type, class, speed, consumption and special features as well as current market prices I consider the vessel's value in undamaged condition in 19 . . [1] to be . . . . . .

1. The request for valuation will at least in general average cases come quite some time after "the termination of the adventure". It is therefore important to have the particular date or period indicated on the certificate. The expert should not use the hindsight acquired or take into account extraneous factors of time. *Cf.* AIDE Cambridge, p. 25.

Some certificates will say explicitly "free of chartering commitment" or words to that effect.

The elements enumerated indicate the salient factors that determine the price of the vessel.

The size

That the vessel's tonnage and carrying capacity is of great importance is obvious. The size will tell a prospective buyer if the vessel is at all suited for the trade he is interested in. Does her draught allow her to use the St Lawrence River? Will she fit into the locks of the Panama Canal? Can she go up to Lake Vänern through the Trollhätte Canal? Regardless of such particular requirements the size will give an indication of her carrying capacity. Is it of the size the prospective buyer is looking for?

The type

The type will determine how a vessel can be used. Is it a tanker, an ore-bulk-oil (OBO) carrier, a reefer, an ordinary dry cargo ship, a roll-on, roll-off vessel? Is it the type the buyer is looking for? When he indicated his interest it is for the shipbroker to bring the buyer and the seller together and find the price on which they will agree. If it is a question of issuing a valuation certiticate the shipbroker, wearing the hat of the official valuer, will indicate the value he believes to be realistic.

The age

With age, the upkeep of the vessel becomes more costly. Deterioration sets in. The equipment, modern at the time the vessel was new, is not necessarily so any more. In some countries vessels become obsolete earlier than in others. In others, shipowners are able to run second-hand and rather old tonnage with profit. Some ports may be closed to vessels beyond a certain age, as well as some open ship's register.[2] Traditionally ships are regarded as feminine. In the

2. Twenty years is the maximum age allowed for entry in the register of Vanuatu (formerly the New Hebrides). See Vincent K Hubbard, "Registration of a Vessel under Vanuatu Law," *Journal of Maritime Law and Commerce*, Vol. 13, No 2, January 1982, p. 235.

circumstances I do not think it necessary to enlarge upon the influence to age in this connection.[3]

Class condition and upkeep

In order to retain her class the vessel undergoes survey according to the classification regulations that apply. Unless the classification society agrees to a system of continuous survey[4] of each part of the vessel in rotation over a five-year period the vessel undergoes special survey every four years. The shipowner often asks for a postponement which may be granted up to 12 months.[5] At the end of the four or five-year period the special survey will probably result in work to be carried out by a shipyard bringing about costs of detention as well. Unless the vessel is running under a continuous survey system this means that work for the retention of her class will have accumulated at the end of each period, and naturally even more so at the end of a second period than at the first. If the vessel has recently renewed her

3. *Cf.* as to age N Mostert in an article about supertankers in *The New Yorker* 13 May 1974, p. 45 *et seq.* "There is an accepted life span for every ship, a period at the end of which the vessel is considered to have no further commercial usefulness—to have paid for itself, earned profits, and contributed to the corporate-tax position of its own replacement value through depreciation—and may finally bring in some money through its scrap or resale value. The write-off life of most supertankers is ten years. This is about half of what is considered normal for tankers in the past, and most ships have gone on for much longer. It is not uncommon for passenger liners to go on well beyond their fortieth birthday . . . cargo ships used to go on even longer than passenger ships, and until recently, it was not unusual to find steamships of seventy or eighty years still trading around European coasts (p. 78) . . . At five years old many supertankers are at the halfway point of their write-off-lives . . . (p. 84). Holding such a ship together beyond the five years point can be onerous, but doing so after ten years could be nightmarish. That is when supertankers will start changing hands. Inevitably they will pass on to some flag-of-convenience owner who would not be buying them if his standards were strict (p. 89)".

Whether this last allegation is true or not in respect of supertankers and *mutatis mutandis* in respect of dry cargo ships I am not prepared to say.

Cf. "Is it likely that the new breed of VLCCs (Very Large Crude Carriers) will have an operating life of 20 years? How many may not survive the critical examination of third survey, let alone the requirement for them in 15 to 20 years' time." G H Dodsworth in "Package deals and syndicates", paper read before Seatrade Money and Ship's Conference 26 March 1973.

4. Classification Regulations, *Lloyd's Register of Shipping* 806. "Continuous Surveys when, at the request of Owners, it has been agreed by the Committee that the complete survey of the hull may be carried out on the Continuous Survey basis, all compartments of the hull should be opened for survey and testing in rotation with an interval of 5 years . . ."

5. Ibid. "803 Special surveys. All steel ships classed with the Society are also subjected to Special Surveys in accordance with the requirements set forth in . . . These surveys become due at 4 yearly intervals, the first 4 years from the date of build or date of Special Survey for Classification, and thereafter 4 years from the date of the previous Special Survey."

class then work for her upkeep is not imminent. All this will have a bearing on the price. There are other considerations to the problem of upkeep to be taken into account. The prospective buyer may be aware that the sellers are well known for the way they keep their vessels in good repair, or that their reputation in that respect is indifferent. While the requirements of the different classification societies probably do not differ very much on paper it is nevertheless a fact that in practice some have a better reputation than others. Not only the vigilance of the classification societies is of interest. The inspections and requirements of the governmental inspectorate may be different in country X and Y. If they are on the low side the inspection of the vessel to be made by the buyer will have to be thorough. The wish to safeguard against disagreeable suprises will have a bearing on the market price obtainable.

Speed

The propelling machinery and its power affect the speed of the vessel. The type of the propelling machinery has a role of its own. Is it a well known type tested as reliable over the years in numerous vessels? Are spare parts readily available? The power will say something about fuel consumption and the running costs per day, about the capacity to keep up speed in adverse conditions, about capacity of manoeuvring where there is ice. Speed is no doubt the most important factor in this connection. It enables the buyer to estimate the number of voyages the vessel will be able to perform during a certain period for the trade for which she is intended. Speed and fuel consumption are closely connected.[6] Slow speed uses less fuel. The prospective buyer will weigh the price of the fuel against the number of round voyages the speed will allow the vessel to perform.

Oil consumption

The text of the valuation certificates shown in the first edition did not specially indicate the word "consumption", i.e. ship's consumption of

6. *Cf.* in this connection T Macduff of the Bureau Veritas who pointed out at the Seatrade Money and Ship's Conference in 1974 in the discussions that followed the paper read by P S Douglas on "Finance and the future of the supertanker" that by reducing the average speed of transportation by 2 knots on a very large ship, one saved 30% of the power of the main engines. For a VLCC this would amount to a saving of some $200,000 a year. "That is not a big saving in money, but it is significant . . . running one's machinery at 30% reduced power means it will not go wrong so easily."

bunker oil and diesel oil. The oil embargo of October/November 1973 and the ensuing remarkable rise in oil prices[7] made ship's consumption of oil an important element in the operation of the ship and in assessing ship's value.

Cargo space, loading and discharging gear

To obtain a true picture of the usefulness of the vessel it is important to know how much cargo she can carry and if this cargo can be loaded, stowed and discharged with ease. Is she a shelterdecker? Does she have large holds with as few bulkheads as permitted by the classification society? What is the available height for the ferry decks if she is intended to run on that sort of line? How many trucks and containers can she carry and up to what height can they be received on board with ease. Does the vessel carry cranes and winches that can take on board her cargo without difficulty? Do any of them have heavy lift character? Is she of a roll-on, roll-off type? The sophisticated gears of the vessel will have a value increasing effect provided they can be used in the ports where her trade is likely to bring her. To a prospective buyer the type and quantity of cargo the vessel is fit to carry and the means to load and discharge efficiently is of great importance.

Refrigerating machinery

If the vessel is specially designed and fitted for carrying refrigerated cargo the type of that machinery and the insulation is important to know. Is it a standard type with a good record elsewhere or an experimental one? Vessels not built for the reefer trade may well have some insulated cargo space intended for cold storage. Details about it are not without interest.

Cost of newbuilding

To take into account only the particulars of an existing type of vessel as enumerated above is not enough to get an overall picture of the

7. Before the oil embargo the standard price for bunker oil was some US$80 and for diesel oil about $118 a ton. In 1980 the prices were $180 (+125%) and $350 (+197%) respectively. At the time of writing (September 1985) the bunker oil price is $150 (+87.5%) and the price for diesel oil $230 (+95%). In March 1986 the trend was different, fuel oil costing US$90 and diesel oil US$190. *Cf.* penultimate paragraph of Preface.

market situation. At least two more elements have a say, the cost of newbuilding and the time it would take to obtain delivery. The price paid or agreed to be paid to the shipyard at the delivery may represent the prevailing tonnage prices at that time. This is not always so. In the comparatively long period between the signing of the contract and the delivery of the new vessel tonnage prices may have gone up or down, and several times at that, whereas there is no doubt when this is written that the shipyard's production costs will have gone up. Whether the shipyard was able when signing the contract to have an index clause inserted in it will depend on whether there was a seller's or a buyer's market at the time. Periods where ships are delivered at a loss to the shipyard are followed by those where the price obtained is well above the tonnage prices on delivery.[8] In between come spells where both parties are happy!

Construction prices, the contractual clauses that go with it and the prospective time of delivery are significant elements that have an overall influence in assessing the market value of a vessel.

Specialized vessels

The description given of the factors that together make up ship's market price is still not complete. The specialized vessels, say a combined passenger and car ferry for a short distance trade, is less attractive on the general market than ordinary tonnage. To find the proper purchaser may well be difficult. On the other hand, if found he may be extremely keen on having, say, a ferry available for the line he is running or about to start. The broker will have to locate a prospective buyer and to evaluate the vessel with particular regard to its value to the prospective buyer of that particular ferry.

In some cases he will be at a loss to find something that represents a market value of the specialized vessel because owing to the type of vessel involved there is none.

There are other examples. What importance should be given to the price obtained at a forced sale?[9] What is the market value of a lightship or a warship? Even the most versatile shipbroker will be at a loss to give the answer. The cairns referred to above in the section on values in general are not there to guide the expert valuer. He may

8. Examples that illustrate building prices as compared with tonnage values appear in the section on hull insurance when discussing claims under an open policy and the provisions in the Swedish Insurance Act, Art. 37.

9. The answer varies as will be seen presently in the chapters on Salvage and General Average.

nevertheless be called upon to give an estimate, e.g. because there is to be a sale in bankruptcy and a minimum price must be fixed, or because the tax authorities have an interest in knowing about the value or because a claim for collision recovery is being prepared. In such cases the guidelines to follow may well be to start out from the building costs and make a yearly deduction of a certain percentage, 10 or more as the case may be.

Ship's value in damaged condition

The lists circulated between shipowners about vessels that are on the market and about prices obtained deal with ships in sound condition. Sometimes ships are put up for sale in damaged condition because owners or hull underwriters think the cost of repairs prohibitive. The ship is offered for sale "as is". A thorough inspection of the damage may have been made and tenders for repairs invited. Those tenders may in fact have induced the sale. Or the sellers have not gone into the details of the damage, leaving this for the prospective buyers to do. What is the market value for a damaged ship? In principle it should be her market value in sound condition as explained above, less the cost of repairs. If these are but vaguely known and a result of a rough estimate the value obtained will contain speculative elements. If the buyer is a shipyard well conversant with the type of vessel involved, then they will have special facilities to effect repairs. Is the aim of the prospective buyer to use the vessel for a particular trade where some of the original equipment and arrangements may be indispensable? Those situations may bring about a higher price than would follow from the standard rule indicated. If the ship is so damaged that she is a wreck or nearly so she will probably be sold for breaking up purposes, the price obtained being her scrap value only. In the section on salvage some examples will illustrate this particular aspect.

The market value

The factors enumerated so far will enable a prospective buyer to place the vessel in the proper pigeonhole. The most important element remains the general market value for tonnage in the world at large. Is there at the time a surplus of empty tonnage on the market waiting for employment? Or is there a shortage of tonnage? Are the dry cargo liners in demand or the OBO carriers? What is the situation in the tanker market?[10] What are the prices obtained recently for similar vessels? What is the general trend of the freight market? How does it affect the type of vessel involved? What influence does the general business climate have on tonnage values?[11]

The broker is aware of all these elements when acting for the seller or buyer as the case may be. He will advise his client about it. The time of delivery is obviously of importance too. He will be able to tell that if the vessel is sold with delivery at Y at the end of the present month the seller should hold out for a price of XYZ. To know the market and its tendencies in the overall field is the professional talent of the broker, acquired after long experience. There may be particular trades where the specialist broker may be the greater authority. The assessment of the "trend of the market" is no exact science, it is rather a knack of the professional man, the broker. His knowledge and the figure on which the parties will agree will be the price obtained and will influence the value of a similar vessel in a valuation certificate.

Rather than make the evaluation of the ship depend on the fingertip feeling of the experienced broker efforts are made in some quarters to rationalize the procedure. The situation in Japan will show what I mean. When assessing ship's value for collision, salvage or general average purposes the licensed valuers[12] proceed by stages using as basis for their calculations (a) the actual cost of newbuilding, (b) the depreciation. When the valuers consider it necessary to do so they take into consideration as subsidiary factors (i) the maintenance of the vessel; (ii) the actual recent sales of similar vessels; and (iii) the general situation on the freight market. The depreciation is arrived at by using statistics, renewed every third year, based on *Fairplay's* information about the actual usage periods for various kinds of vessels. Ten per cent is taken as the scrap value and 100% as the costs of newbuilding. The intermediate points are found by plotting into the statistics actual sales and drawing a curve from which the average real depreciation can be read.

---

10. The fluctuations in the market are illustrated by the following: "That black cloud blotting out the sun in which almost every shipowner has basked for more than a year is made up of expert reports forecasting the biggest tanker surplus on record, with at least £1 billion worth of shipping idle during the next couple of years" *The Economist* 18-24 May 1974.

11. Political blacklisting of a ship is "in principle" attached to the ship itself and should have a bearing on her market value if applied to the letter.

12. There are three licensed valuers in Japan, The Japan Shipping Exchange, The Nippon Kaiji Kentei Kyokai and the Shin Nihon Kentei Kyokai (New Japan Surveyors and Sworn Measurers Association).

Guidelines like those indicated are not a common feature.[13] Elsewhere the professional knowledge of the shipbroker, perhaps in conjunction with a surveyor or naval architect, will prevail. (See Chapter 4.) But such an assessment may be challenged in court. The attorney for the defence in a collision case will not necessarily accept a claim based on a valuation certificate by the expert valuer, official or not. He will call him as an expert witness and put his knowledge to the test. In assessing ship's market value at the relevant time how far back did you look for deals with similar vessels? Was it a week, a fortnight or more? Even sister ships are hardly of the same age; when making comparisons with other deals how did you account for the difference in size, speed, age, etc.? Did you take into account the recent increase (fall) in the rate of interest? Did the trade unions' attitude towards seamen's wages for vessels sailing under flags of convenience influence your assessment? Did you take into account the repercussions of the 1973 oil crisis in your assessment?[14] The Suez Canal was closed (was reopened). Hostilities between X and Y have broken out (have come to an end). These events are bound to influence the freight market. What impact did they have on the valuation you indicate? You are aware that at the relevant time the vessel was lying in Z. Did that have any bearing on your assessment?[15]

13. *Cf.* in this connection 1972 AMC, p. 627 (USDC, SDNY). The ferryboat *Orange*, *Miles* v. *Rosenthal*. The ferryboat was bought for $2,850 and insured for $100,000; her estimated cost of reproduction was $750,000 and the estimated market value $100,000. The surveyor to the US Salvage Association said that for valuation purposes use had been made of information in the Association's file concerning similar vessels, . . . "the United States Salvage Association Inc. frequently performed surveys for underwriters to determine the 'fair insurance value' of a vessel. Such valuations were commonly designed as 'market value'. Whether or not actually predicated on sale's date . . . while the Association in making valuation of a vessel frequently consults data pertaining to sale's prices of vessels similar to that being surveyed, if available, another method of determining value for insurance purposes is costs of reconstruction less straight line of depreciation. That was the method . . . used in valuing the *Orange* at $100,000." *Cf.* *American Mail Line* v. *Skagit River Navigation & Trading Co* AMC 1375, 91 F (2d) 835, 844, 45 (9th Cir. 1937). In the *Orange* case the court accepted a definition of market value different from the definition used by the Supreme Court in *The Proteus* v. *Cushing* (see above p. 7).

14. The oil embargo came into effect in October/November 1973. The repercussions on prices of dry cargo ships were felt as soon as January 1974, while for tankers in the autumn of that year (*cf.* above p. 26).

15. This last question draws attention to the situation where a ship when sold is lying at a place definitely off the beaten track. The prospective buyer will have to bring her to a commercially more attractive place. He may let the costs of the ballast voyage influence the price he is prepared to pay. Parallels, for what they are worth, may be drawn from the provisions and discussions on redelivery of the vessel in a time

These are some of the questions that may be put and the answers to them all have a bearing on the market value. For instance, to make the time element fit into a strict formula is not possible except that a sale before any of the events indicated above will have lost much of its significance even if made shortly before. The court will get the overall impression that the various elements the attorney wanted to pinpoint all go into a "basket" and that it is difficult to be too precise as to the influence of the one or the other on the market value indicated by the expert valuer.

Restricted market

The description of how the market price of the vessel is arrived at and the elements that go into it are based on the conditions in a free market. The situation will be different if the authorities step in and issue regulations. They may say that a vessel may not be sold abroad without a special licence. This may in some cases make it more difficult for the seller to obtain the best price possible owing to the uncertainty as to whether a licence will be granted or not. They may introduce maximum freights for vessels flying their flags. Or the authorities may fix a ceiling price for vessels. This did happen in Norway in 1940. The Norwegian Government declared that no Norwegian vessels were to be sold for a price above that which existed on 8 April 1940, the day before the occupation of Norway by German forces. Although the provisions did not apply to sales abroad it would appear that it had the effect that practically no voluntary sales or purchases took place during the period that the enactment was in force.[16]

The situation where ship's prices are regulated by official enactments are of course not confined to the examples given. Take France, where owners, owing to currency restrictions after the Second World War, could not obtain a licence to buy foreign ships. They were compelled to buy French ones, which made the value of a ship much higher in France than in the international market.[17] During the

charterparty (See H P Michelet: "Periodens lengde ved tidscertepartier," *Arkiv for Sjørett*, Vol. 11 Oslo 1971–72, p. 590 *et seq.* esp. p. 646). Particular aspects of the geography problems are discussed when dealing with salvage, general average and restricted market.

16. Reference is made to the discussion about the effect of these regulations by Thorbjörnsen, p. 276 *et seq.* See also discussion under the collision recovery section.

17. Questionnaire, part of the preparatory work of the 1962 CMI Conference in Athens, designated as *Dom.* 5 in the English version (not in print).

Second World War the War Shipping Administration of the USA requisitioned merchant vessels. The US Government also embarked on a large building programme. In 1946 the vessels were returned to their original owners. For the huge number of vessels built by the US Government a Ship Sales Act was passed in order to facilitate the transfer to private ownership of the competitively useful portion of them.[18] The Act provided for elaborate formulas with floors and ceilings for arrival at sales price. I quoted from a commentator:

"The effect of this Act and its valuation formulas on the valuing of ships for general average and salvage purposes, while seemingly definite on some types of ships of which there was a pool available if purchasers came forward in sufficient number to take them up at prices established by the Act, seems only to confuse the problem further on other types. It must be remembered that as asking price is one thing and a bid price another, and that some types are simply not available . . . It would be difficult indeed to see how the Ship Sale Act Valuation formulas could be applied to vessels so scarce in number as not to be readily deliverable to buyers at those prices and as to justify continued construction at costs practically triple basic prices established in the Act . . . On some types it has seemed safe to insure on single valuations based on Ship Sales Act values and/or Maritime Commission requirements. On other dual valuations or alternatively excess liability coverage have been resorted to."[19]

Where the market economy prevails official enactments to regulate ship's price or the export of vessels are sometimes introduced as emergency measures and abolished when the special situation is no longer at hand. This is not necessarily so everywhere. In those countries that apply the planned state economy the situation may be different. I draw attention, as an example, to the situation in the German Democratic Republic. A ship built in that country and bought from its shipping enterprises will fall into the category of *Fixed prices* (Festpreise). The actual building cost is the basis for finding the price . . . "indirectly the international market value is also reflected up to a certain extent by such inland prices".[20] I understand this to mean that while the contracted price will constitute the basic value a

18. The *Dom.* 5 says attention is drawn to a salvage where the owner of a Liberty ship flying the American flag could take advantage of the American legislation according to which such a ship at the time of the salvage could be bought in the USA for a sum nearly half her value on the international market.

19. Warren G Springer as Chairman of the Association of Average Adjusters of the United States in his address to that Association 1946.

20. I am indebted to Dr Dolly Richter-Hannes of the Association for Maritime Law of the German Democratic Republic, Rostock, for these comments and information.

steep rise or fall in ship's values in the international market may be allowed to influence the price to a certain extent.[21]

The market value and the charterparty

The charterparty problems in connection with the assessment of ship's value will be discussed in the following section. In the circumstances it is sufficient to say here that a prospective buyer and seller will have to take into account a charterparty. Is it a low rate or high rate one? Will the ship be sold with or without it? How much time remains of an unfulfilled time charter contract? How many consecutive voyages are to be performed under the chartering agreement in force? How much time remains before the ship becomes free of commitments? Will the charterer accept a new owner?[22] Is the charterer financially reliable?

21. These are examples of where the market becomes restricted because of measures taken from outside. It would be equally true to use the term where highly specialized vessels, say a railway ferry, are to be sold. The restriction is inherent in the subject matter itself and the "market" has lost its true meaning also in that case.

22. The contractual agreements embodied in the charterparty are no secret between the seller and the buyer. They may, as indicated, influence the price depending *inter alia* on whether charterers are prepared to accept the prospective new owner as their contractual partner. What about the type of claims against the vessel as are secured by a lien on the ship, sometimes described as the silent rights? They remain valid after a voluntary sale of the ship. Will they influence the price the buyer is ready to pay? They will, I should say, provided of course he is or is made aware of them. If unknown to the buyer at the time of the transaction he is probably left with a right of action for damages against the seller for non-disclosure of material facts, for what that is worth.

6

Influence of the Charterparty on Ship's Value

Introduction

A number of questions come under this heading. Does a time charter, a bare boat charter or a charter for consecutive voyages influence ship's value to her owner? If it does, in what way: increasing or reducing her value? The terms of the charterparty will give the answer. Are the number of vessels under charter sufficient to warrant that attention is devoted to the influence, if any, of a charterparty on ship's value. If charterparties do influence ship's value are they taken into account when assessing ship's value? Does a charterparty automatically follow the ship if sold? If it does not should a change be advocated?

The first difficulty to overcome when dealing with these problems is to decide whether to deal with them together under one heading or to treat them separately in the sections on collision, salvage, etc., where the practical impact of the charterparty is felt.

I have opted in favour of treating the charterparty questions under one heading. This assertion is, however, subject to important reservations. The survival of the charterparty as a *de lege ferenda* problem I discuss under the section on ship's value for credit purposes which I think is the proper place for it. The evaluation of assessing ship's value "with commitments", i.e. including her charterparty, I take up in the sections on collision and salvage and also in connection with general average where the practical effect becomes tangible.

(a) *Does a charterparty influence ship's value to her owner?*

The answer to this question is: it may well do. If a ship is under a profitable charterparty of some duration she will be more valuable to her owner as a going concern than if she is tied up by a poor charterparty or is a free ship.

In *The Castor*[1] a salvage case, ship's value free of commitments was

---

1. *The Castor* (1932) 18 Asp. MLC 312.

34

assessed at £72,820 whereas the agreed duration of the charterparty made the value of the vessel to her owners £85,000. The practical effects of the charterparty (based on the assumption that it could be made to follow the ship or be renegotiated on identical terms) is explained in another case as follows:

The time between the last day of discharge (the relevant date for general average purposes) of the vessel A and the termination of her time charter period was 302 days. Her net earning under the charter was £323 a day or for the remaining 302 days   £97,546
   The freight rate underwent a change.
If the vessel A was chartered at her last day of discharge her net
earning under such a charter would have been only £80 a day
or for 302 days   – £24,169
                                                                            ―――――――
The balance   £73,386
thus represented the value to the owners of her actual charterparty. The valuers said ship's value in sound and seaworthy condition at the relevant date free of charter was £340,000. This means that if they had added the value of the charterparty to the said value making it £413,386 (or a round figure in that neighbourhood) this would mean an increase of more than 20% over the "free ship value".[2]

These two examples go to show that a profitable charterparty will increase the value of the ship as a going concern to her owner. Likewise a poor charterparty will go to reduce that value. The *San Onofre*[3] was valued at £369,841 whereas if the duration of the low rate contract entered into was taken into account her value was only £160,000. A still more striking example of the effect of a poor charterparty has been given to me, subject to the source not being divulged, where the vessel was valued in the sum of $1.5 million subject to charter and to $49 million free of charter, her current hull insurance valuation being $13.5 million!

   The above examples are sufficient to show two things. First, that to the owner the terms of an affreightment of some duration will make the ship as a going concern more valuable to him, or less, as the case may be. Secondly, that difference in value assessed "with commitments" or as a "free ship" may well be considerable.

2. The example taken from *Protokoll Sjette Nordiske Dispachørsmøde Göteborg,* 1966 (XX: 15), not in print.
3. *The San Onofre* (1917) 17 Asp. MLC, 74.

(b) *Is the number of vessels under charterparty sufficiently large to warrant that attention be devoted to the influence of the charterparty?*

The number of vessels travelling the seas under long time charters, bare boat charters, demise charters and charters for consecutive voyage is hard to assess. It is not possible to give exact figures. What was true yesterday is not necessarily true today and may be completely wrong tomorrow.

With all reservations as to possible mistakes this much can be said. The principal types of vessels in the world fleet mid-1972 according to *Lloyd's Register of Shipping Statistical Tables* 1972 amounted to 57,391. In 1985 the number was 76,068 (+ 18.5%). The gross tonnage in 1972 was 268,340,000 as against 418,682,422 in 1984 (+ 56%).

How many of them performed their voyage under charterparties I asked in the first edition and said that some 12,000 ships out of the total number in 1972, or roughly 20%, were sailing the seas under time charter or voyage charter.[4]

I then tried to draw some conclusions. I quote:

"This rough estimate will not necessarily convey the true overall picture. Lloyd's figures probably make tramp vessels on time charter appear along with general cargo vessels. This would mean that the above figure for chartered vessels may well err on the low side. Even so, it is difficult to draw definite conclusions. The proportion of vessels on long-term charters is changing continually. I had the opportunity of seeing a list of how some 100 ore/oil carriers and about the same number of bulk/oil carriers were employed in one month in 1971 from which it appeared that more than 30 of the first and more than 40 of the second category were chartered for a period of 12 months or more. The world's merchant fleet today, G H Dodsworth said on 26 March 1973,[5] consists of more than 400 million tons deadweight, which is made up of 52% tankers, 23% bulk carriers, 17% dry cargo and the remainder, combination carriers, etc., takes up 8%."

However you look at these figures it is safe to say that while the number of vessels under long time charters varies the number is considerable and still more their size and their value. The number of cases dealt with in the UK where the English approach to ship's value operates is impressive as will be shown by figures submitted in the following sections.

---

4. This figure has since been challenged as being much too low. It was pointed out that a vessel might at the same time be under a bare boat charter, a time charter and a voyage charter.

5. *Cf.* paper by G H Dodsworth referred to in the section on market value.

The plight of the shipping industry in 1985 may have made the figures and perhaps the conclusions about the great numbers of vessels under long time charters irrelevant. I have seen statistics for 1985 about the merchant fleet to the effect that some 80% of it consisted of tankers, bulk carriers and combination carriers and the remaining 20% of container ships and other types of conventional cargo liners. We know that many tankers were laid up in 1985. We surmise that with the surplus of tonnage in 1985 the number of vessels under charter was proportionally smaller than in 1975. I submit that in spite of a reduced number of vessels being so employed, it is worthwhile to "devote interest to the English method of valuation of ships" because of the principles involved and the practical consequences.

(c) *Are charterparties taken into account when assessing ship's value?*
  (i) *Situation outside England*

The instructions issued by the Swedish Maritime Board[6] say in Art 15:

"In assessing the value of a vessel regard should be had for, *inter alia*, vessel's age, type, class, running costs, speed, equipment for its intended purposes; general upkeep, whether vessel has undergone important repairs or reconstruction, vessel's general usefulness or usefulness for special trade, general market price for similar vessels and for new such vessels. When in doubt about ship's value special experts should be called upon."

The official Swedish valuers interpret their instructions to mean that in assessing the value of a vessel they should look to her general market value and disregard any charterparty, good or bad, that may attach to the vessel and they invariably do so.

Discussing the situation of ships' value for salvage purposes Braekhus[7] quotes the case of the *Sunlong*, worth Nkr. 3.5 million without her charterparty at the time of the salvage in December 1954, with a profitable charterparty running until November/December 1956 and bought shortly before the accident for Nkr 5.1 million.

After looking into relevant English cases which will be discussed presently he says that although in Norwegian law the situation is not definitely decided, practice, however, points in the direction that it is ship's value free of charter that is relevant in a salvage.

---

6. *Anvisningar för besiktningsmän*, G 70/71 printed 2 December 1970.
7. Sjur Braekhus 747: 1 and 747: 2.

Another Norwegian writer, N Beyer, does not agree.[8] No rule can be laid down, he says, to the effect that time charters shall be disregarded when assessing ship's value for salvage purposes. Information about the contents of the charterparty will always be appropriate as a basic element in the assessment of ship's value. Thus, whereas Braekhus says the situation is not definitely settled but points strongly towards disregarding charterparties, Beyer holds that the situation is unsettled and that charterparties may well have a bearing on the value. I would have thought that there is at least one decision, not referred to by any of them, that gives a clear indication of the attitude of the law in Scandinavia,[9] *The Stigstad* case.[10]

On her voyage from Malmö the Norwegian steamer *Stigstad* grounded in January 1916, and was taken into Gothenburg. Hull underwriters ordered her to Sandefjord in Norway where she was repaired. She was insured for Nkr 1,000,000. Her value in damaged condition was estimated at Nkr 800,000, the cost of repairs at Nkr 426,450 and her value as repaired as Nkr 1,050,000.

A petition for her condemnation was made. As to this petition the court said "that the vessel with reference to the said assessments and taking into account the information in the documents submitted could not be found worth repairing, which the Court finds already appears indirectly from the said assessment". Hull underwriters accepted the verdict and paid for total loss and had the vessel struck from the register. They took over the vessel and sold her to a new owner. Her name was then *Tripel*. She was torpedoed and sunk in the autumn of 1916. According to a charterparty dated 8 February 1910 a Canadian company had chartered the *Stigstad* for the St Lawrence seasons 1912 to 1919 at a rate of 3s 6d per ton. In arriving at the value in sound condition and also in her damaged condition, the court of first instance took into consideration this charterparty. When the ship was condemned her owners then informed the brokers of the Canadian company about the condemnation and said that the charterparty they had entered into with the Canadian company had come to an end. The company did not accept this and took exception to the condemnation. It challenged the decision of the Norwegian court. The case eventually came before the Norwegian Supreme Court. The Supreme Court considered the point whether a charterparty should be allowed to influence the value of the ship as assumed by the court below. The Supreme Court said it should not and explained that when in the "travaux préparatoires" to the relevant Article in the Maritime Code (Art 6) it is said that every circumstance should be taken into account in the case at hand this means obviously the character of the vessel or the state of the

8. Introduction to seminar of Scandinavian Institute of Maritime Law 13 April 1966, not in print.
9. Wherever similar legislation is at hand, as in the maritime field, Scandinavian courts pay much attention to decisions reached in the other Nordic countries.
10. ND 1917, p. 81.

market. But "every circumstance", the Supreme Court goes on to say, "cannot be understood to mean any charterparty that may have been made in respect of the ship nor any other contracts made in respect of it like say bunkering contracts. Such contracts are only of importance to the profitability of the ship but has nothing to do with ship's value . . . As it is thus an established fact that the charterparty has influenced the assessment of values made and the condemnation and that it is not in accordance with the provisions of the law to give to the charterparty such influence these decisions by the Maritime Court must be without relevance to the appellant unless other circumstances indicate that the appellant should have to abide by them".

The Supreme Court did find that no such circumstances were at hand and set aside the ruling of the court below.

This means, as I understand it, that we have it on high authority in Scandinavia that no contract attaching to the ship, whether charterparties or not, shall be allowed to influence ship's value. Thus the views expressed by Braekhus, with which I agree, that charterparties good or poor should not be taken into account, are vindicated.

I have not been able to trace, either in legal writing or by personal contacts, any information tending to disprove that ship's value free of commitments is the accepted basis for assessment of ship's value everywhere outside England.

(ii) *Situation in England*

I will have to devote much attention to the particular situation in England and to some extent in the USA.

Much as I would like to sum up the situation in a few succinct sentences I feel I am unable to do so. "The value to her owners as a going concern" and words to that effect are sometimes hard to pinpoint as to their true meaning.

In *The Hohenzollern*[11] the defendants in a salvage case argued that the objective value should be used. The appraisers, they said, had based their valuation of the vessel on the value to her owners. In doing so they had followed *The Harmonides*[12] but that was an erroneous view to take; the proper basis on which valuation should be made should be the market value of the vessel. This view the court rejected: "The value is what she is worth in her damaged state to her owners. That is

---

11. *The Hohenzollern* (1906) 10 Asp. MLC 236.
12. *The Harmonides* (1903) 9 Asp. MLC 334.

the view the court will take in the future so the appraisement in this case will be accepted."

In *The San Onofre*[13] the salved value to her owners was £160,000 and the Admiralty Marshal's valuation was £369,849, the difference being due to the vessel having been chartered for 16 years at a low rate of hire. There the President (Sir Samuel Evans) said.[14]

"In no case so far as I am aware have the charters of a vessel been taken into account in assessing the value of the salved ship in salvage proceedings, and I think it would be very undesirable from all points of view if there should be introduced into valuations in salvage cases any element of that kind, which would make a reference to the Register and Merchants necessary in order to ascertain the value of the salved ship.

The ship is salved and may be arrested as she is, as the salvors are entitled to arrest the *res*. If bail is not given the ship may be sold. She would not be sold subject to charterparties, but as she existed to anyone who wanted to buy a ship of her description.

In this case an undertaking was given in ordinary form; and the Writ as issued was directed to the owners of the *San Onofre* her cargo and freight and all other persons interested in the vessel. The Court has nothing to do with the relationship between the shipowners and the charterers; nor in my opinion have the salvors to do with any such question."

In the salvage case of *The Castor*[15] (incidentally a Swedish vessel) the fact that the vessel was at the time of the services under a profitable and unexpired time charterparty was taken into account and the present value of future earnings under such charterparty was included in the appraised value. Lord Merrivale said *inter alia*.

"So far as I am able to see there is nothing in the case of the *San Onofre* which in any way infringes or was intended to infringe the principle laid down in the case of the *Hohenzollern*."

Then there is the case of *The Edison*[16] that went to the House of Lords. A dredger, the *Liesboch*, was sunk by the *Edison* and it was said that the plaintiffs were entitled to the value of the dredger as a going concern at the time and place of the loss. This was explained by Lord Wright, who said *inter alia*.[17]

"The true rule seems to be that the measure of damages in such cases is the value of the ship to her owner as a going concern at the time and place of the loss. In assessing that value regard must naturally be had to her pending

13. *The San Onofre* (1917) 17 Asp. MLC 74.
14. *Ibid.*, at p. 96.
15. *The Castor* (1932) 18 Asp. MLC 312.
16. *The Edison* (1933) 18 Asp. MLC 380; 42 Ll.L.Rep 23.
17. Commercial Cases Vol. XXXVIII, p. 274/275.

engagements, either profitable or the reverse. The rule, however, obviously requires some care in its application; the figure of damage is to represent the capitalized value of the vessel as a profit-earning machine, not in the abstract but in view of the actual circumstances. The value of prospective freights cannot simply be added to the market value, but ought to be taken into account in order to ascertain the total value for purpose of the damage, since if it is merely added to the market of a free ship the owner will be getting *pro tanto* his damages twice over. The vessel cannot be earning in the open market while fulfilling the pending charter or charters. Again, the present valuation of a future charter becomes a matter of difficulty in the case even of successive charters, still more in the case of long charters—such, for instance, as that in the *Lord Strathcona Steamship Company* v. *Dominion Coal Company*,[17a] which was for ten St Lawrence seasons, with extension at the charterers' option for further eight seasons. The assessment of the value of such a vessel at the time of loss, with her engagements, may seem to present an extremely complicated and speculative problem. But different considerations apply to the simple case of a ship sunk by collision when free of all engagements either being laid up in port or being a seeking ship in ballast, though intended for employment, if it can be obtained, under charter or otherwise. In such a case the fair measure of damage will be simply the market value, on which will be calculated the interest at and from the date of loss, to compensate for delay in paying for the loss. But the contrasted cases of a tramp under charter or a seeking tramp do not exhaust all the possible problems in which must be sought an answer to the question what is involved in the principle *restitutio in integrum*. I have only here mentioned such cases as the step to considering the problem in the present case. Many, varied, and complex are the types of vessels and the modes of employment in which their owners may use them. Hence the difficulties constantly felt in defining rules as to the measure of damages. I think it impossible to lay down any universal formula. A ship of war, a supply ship, a lightship, a dredger employed by a public authority, a passenger liner, a trawler, a cable ship, a tug boat (to take a few instances)—all may raise quite different questions before their true value can be ascertained."

What have legal writers said in this respect?

"The value of the ship", Kennedy says,[18] "is her value to her owners as a going concern. In arriving at the value contractual engagements of the ship are taken into account as one element of value."

"The value of the ship", says Scrutton LJ, "is an estimate, or rough capitalisation of the earning power of the ship for its life. If, therefore, for example, the ship is under charter for ten years, that fact has to be considered in fixing the value of the ship as a going concern. It follows that profits under a valuable charter cannot be added to the value of the ship to her owners as a going concern because that would be giving the same amount twice."

17a. (1925) 23 Ll.L.Rep 145; [1926] A.C. 108.
18. W R Kennedy, p. 276, note 15. The very full reference of cases cites the cases of *The Harmonides* (1903), *The Hohenzollern* (1906), *The Castor* (1932), *The Edison* (1933) already referred to and *The Kate* (1899) 8 Asp. MLC 539.

Commenting on *The San Onofre* case Kennedy is sceptical that the decision was intended to limit the operation of the earlier decision, especially as Lord Merrivale in the *Castor* case saw no conflict between them.

To Carver[19] there is a conflict of authority, whether in assessing the salved value of a ship a charterparty should be taken into account or not.

"In *The San Onofre* in which the ship was chartered for the next sixteen years at a low rate Evans P held that her charter should not be taken into account in assessing her value. But Lord Merrivale P held otherwise in *The Castor* case in which the ship was under a profitable time charter. In such a case it might be better, however, to consider the benefit under the time charter as freight salved, rather than to include it in the value of the ship."

J G R Griggs[20] says:

"Although Lord Merrivale in *The Castor* found grounds for distinguishing his decision from that of *The San Onofre* the fact of the matter is that he was disagreeing with *The San Onofre* decision, and as the law now stands, the position is one of 'heads I win, tails you lose', in salvor's favour."

Finally we have R F Olsen[21] who makes an effort to reconcile *The Castor* and *The San Onofre* cases. As in collision cases he says subjective contractual arrangements are admissible only to the extent that they are foreseeable. Thus one can say that *The Castor* is authority for the proposition that it is foreseeable that a vessel may be more valuable as a result of a long time charter, while *The San Onofre* can be cited as authority that it is not forseeable that an unfavourable charterparty might reduce the value of a ship to her owner.

He is not satisfied with that explanation and tries another saying: "that the value for salvage purposes is to be reached by a modified

---

19. *Carver*, para. 1315, p. 452.

20. J G R Griggs: "Aspects of salvage". *Il Diritto Marittimo*, Genova 1965 reproducing a paper read before the Institute of London Underwriters in December 1963.

Sense of logic is commonly ascribed to the Latin people. An example of it is found in the arbitration by Ferrarini in the salvage case of *The Lykaion* (18 December 1972; *Il Diritto Marittimo* 1972, p. 655 *et seq.*). The salvors contended that ship's value was some six to seven million dollars. The arbitrator, having investigated the charterparty conditions and the period for which the *Lykaion* was committed, found that the freight was well below the freight rates prevailing at the time of the salvage. He therefore concludeed that the *Lykaion* had a value that was about one half of the market price for a similar vessel free of commitments. According to information obtained by the arbitrator, arbitrators in England had valued the ship at £1,500,000 or $3,600,000 a value agreed upon by the owners of the *Lykaion* and the Greek salvors (there were others as well). This he thought was a realistic value and the one to be used.

21. "The Value of the Salved Ship", in *Arkiv for Sjørett*, Vol. 12, pp. 215–236.

market test, in which one can take the owner's subjective position into account. Thus if it appears that a vessel is worth more to her owner by reason of his contractual commitments, then that value is to be taken, but, if his contractual commitments make her worth less to him than the price that the vessel would realise on the open market, then her market value is to be taken."

He does not like that either and in the end opts for "the suggestion made by Carver to regard the benefit under the charter, in such a case as *The Castor*, as freight salved, rather than as part of the value of the ship".

Now that all the material is there it is time to try to answer the question whether the charterparty is taken into account when assessing ship's value under English law.

My understanding is that profitable long term charters will be made to add to ship's value in salvage cases and probably also in collision cases; although the increased value may there appear in the shape of freight interest. It is more difficult to say for certain that a poor long time charter will make the assessment go below ship's ordinary market value. There may be a difference in this respect between salvage and collision cases and in *The Edison*, a collision case, no doors were closed or at any rate locked. I have had confirmed for this edition that the position in English law is still that charterparties must be taken into account in assessing ship's value. Unprofitable charterparties could have the effect of reducing ship's value below the charterparty free market value but never below the scrap value because the charterparty would then be frustrated.[22]

22. It is a matter of speculation what an English court would make of the situation where the vessel is under a leasing contract that may constitute a hire-purchase contract with a transfer of ownership to take place at an agreed date.

As for leasing problems in connection with vessel see "Nature juridique du contrat de leasing pour les navires" by M Pape, Berlin and DC Richter-Hannes, Rostock in "Droit Maritime Français", 1973, p. 837 and the legal authors referred to in that study.

I do not go into the leasing problem in this study about ship's value. I am prepared to agree with B Quick who said in a paper called "Market Conditions and the availability of money" read before the Seatrade Money and Ship's Conference on 2 April 1974: "The leasing of ships is a complicated subject . . . It can be very satisfactory as far as rate, term and percentage are concerned, but the majority of owners do not like the prospect of a vessel being owned by another party."

Seen from the angle of ship's value, leasing is of interest mainly as an insurance problem, that is to say what party should insure what interest in the ship. In his book *Leie av Skib*, Oslo 1969 T Falkanger takes up the insurance problems connected with chartering under §§ 32: 7 and 32: 8. Some useful parallels could probably be drawn from it in respect of leasing and insurance.

(iii) *Situation in the USA*

Is the situation in the USA the same as in Scandinavia and elsewhere outside of England? I would have thought so. "It has never been the practice to take into consideration any charterparty—whether it be remunerative or otherwise."[23] This sounds pretty clear. Still in a study of this kind it is necessary to look into the situation more closely. We have *The Kia Ora*, a salvage case (252 Fed. 507; 4th Cir. 1918). There ship's value free of charter was $3 million. She was requisitioned by the British Government under a time charter which made her actual market value only $1,772,600. "It seems clear" the court said, "that the real value as property found by the District Court was her actual condition of requisition, not what would have been her value with that condition removed."[23a] The lower value of $1,772,600 was the proper value for salvage purposes.

To me the relevant factor appears to be that the *Kia Ora* was requisitioned, thus rather an illustration of governmental restriction than the impact of the poor charterparty.[24] Moreover the case is over 50 years old, with to my knowledge no successors, and is no firm ground for an assertion that in the USA the poor charterparty will be allowed to reduce ship's value in salvage cases.

I think it is correct to say that under the law of the USA a charterparty will not enhance or diminish the value of a vessel[25]

23. Buglass 2nd edn., p. 182 (3rd edn., p. 272).

23a. *Cf.* Norris/Benedict Vol. 3, A §263 (the work of Norris' having been incorporated in Benedict 7th edn.) who says that the market value of the salved property, when a market value exists, is the most accurate means of determining the salved value based upon actual sales of vessels similar to that of the salved ship. "If the vessel is under restrictions such restrictions must be taken into account before the true market value can be established."

The effect of restriction is illustrated by the two cases of *The Premuda* (1940) 67 Ll.L.Rep 9 and *The Prins Knud* (1940) 67 Ll.L.Rep 458 quoted by I H Wildeboer p. 205. The *Premuda* was an Italian ship the value of which, in sound condition, the court estimated at £75,000. In connection with the restrictions made by the Italian Government and the fact that the owner could not evade them, the value was determined at £55,000. After a deduction of £30,000 for serious damage the salved value was £25,000. The Danish vessel the *Prins Knud* was set at £21,750 assuming that she was an English ship. "Since in 1940 at the time of the salvage, Danish ships had a free market (in contrast to English ships) the court increased the sound value and assessed the value salved at £24,000."

24. To the particular issue of the unfavourable charterparty and the maritime liens resulting from shipowner's breach of contract reference is made in Benedict Vol. 3, §§66, pp. 7–40–7–41 and also Gilmore and Black 744/45.

25. *Cf. Neptune Lines* v. *Hudson Valley* 1973 AMC, 125 (SDNY 1972); *The Fire Island* 1950 AMC 873 (5th Cir. 1950) and *The Tug Huntington*, 1982 AMC 2588 (2nd Cir. 1982). In *The Huntington* case the operation of the vessel at a loss during the year preceeding the collision was considered by the court in assessing the market value.

except that it will indirectly be taken into account by the courts in assessing the market value

This being my appreciation of the situation it follows that the English method of valuation is something apart. There is the proud mother who said: "The whole platoon marches out of step except my John!" That English law is different from the law elsewhere is not without significance as will become apparent, for example, in the section on salvage.

(d) *Does the charterparty automatically follow the ship if sold?*

If the seller, the buyer and the charterer all agree that a change of ownership of the vessel shall not affect the charterparty under which she is sailing this is a contractual agreement between the parties. There is nothing to prevent them from entering into such an agreement. The question put in the heading is different, i.e. would the charterparty follow the ship failing such an agreement? The answer is no, not as the law stands today.[26] In order to displace the adage "Sales breaks hire" some form of registration of the charterparty, like the mortgage in the ship, would be necessary and there is none. This negative answer would be true also in the USA. The lien for breach of contract that under American law follows the vessel into the hands of a *bona fide* purchaser does not mean that the charterparty survives a change of ownership, only that an additional security is given to the claim for damages.

26. In *The Tercero* case (ND 1955, p. 245 *et seq.*) the legal nature of the charterparty received some attention by the courts. The ship was requisitioned by the Norwegian authorities. Charterers sued them, unsuccessfully, for damages following from the loss of the charterparty. The Oslo City Court said in respect of the charterparty that charterers' right according to it was not a right *in rem* but a contractual right. Charterers were no more successful in the Supreme Court. Judge Gundersen giving the verdict of the court said *inter alia* that it was not necessary for him to go into the problem of the legal nature of the charterparty whether this was a purely contractual agreement or whether charterers' rights had more or less the characteristics of a right *in rem* or whether the charterparty was a contract *sui generis*. Still less was he inclined to draw any practical legal conclusions from the systematic aspect that should properly be ascribed to the contract entered into between the shipowner and the charterers. To him it was enough to lay down in this case that under Norwegian law there was no support for giving the charterers a direct claim against the requisitioner when the ship in question was the subject of requisition.

The Tercero case deals in an indirect way only with the nature of the contract embodied in the charterparty. Suffice it to say that the case at any rate lends no support to the concept of charterer's right as a right *in rem* attached to the ship rather as an albeit cautious declaration in favour of the merely contractual nature of the charterparty.

I know of no law system where at present the charterparty automatically follows the ship if sold.[27]

(e) *The survival of the charterparty in case the ship is sold as a de lega ferenda problem*

If it is correct to say that as the law stands today the charterparty will not automatically follow the ship, this does not mean that the problem of whether a change should be introduced has not been discussed. I shall give an *exposé* of those discussions under the section devoted to ship's value for credit purposes. This is because the practical advantages and disadvantages of a survival are best understood in that context. I shall also indicate there my own views in the matter.

(f) *Evaluation of the English valuation method*

In the description of the English valuation system given I have not indicated my own views on the matter. This I will do in the section on collision and on salvage where the evaluation of the practical effects becomes apparent and thus more easy to grasp.

---

27. *Cf.* Braekhus, S in *Kontraktspant i Skip*, p. 189. The time charterparty does not follow the ship unless the charterparty contains a clause that the time charterer is bound to accept a change of ownership.

This study not purporting to embrace the law of charterparties. Suffice it to say here that a number of charterparty clauses have that effect.

7

Ship's Value for Credit Purposes

Introduction

Vessels are becoming more and more expensive. Shipyards the world over will perhaps take exception to this assertion and point out that from time to time they experience periods where the contracted price is totally inadequate to meet rising costs. This is true enough. Still it is a fact that the building prices, seen over a long period, have gone up. There are several reasons. Vessels grow in size. Their equipment becomes more sophisticated. The requirements of the authorities for safety measures become more and more stringent. The costs of the shipyard go up. Inflation is a world-wide feature. It all adds up to make building costs rise. However, a situation with prolonged tonnage surplus will break the upward tendency and the prices asked for by the shipyards for a newbuilding will go down. The price for building an 80,000 ton deadweight tanker was about US$30 million in 1981, some $25 million in 1983 and in 1985 about $21 million, a reduction of 30%. This percentage, striking enough, does not give the true picture because of the currency situation. The US dollar was worth Sw.Kr. 4.39 in January 1981 and Sw.Kr. 9.02 in January 1985. The devaluation of the Swedish krona and the rise of the US dollar transformed the reduction of 30% into an increased price for the Swedish shipowner of some 44%. Customers from other countries have been luckier. Few, if any, shipowners will be able to finance the building of a new vessel of some size without financial backing from the outside.

Nobody will object to what has been said so far, but some may say that no legal aspects are involved that motivate a place for ship's value for credit purposes in a study devoted to legal problems. I make no excuses for bringing the matter in. First of all there are legal problems involved and I shall try to explain what they are. Secondly, it would be odd in a legal study on ship's value to exclude an important topic in maritime affairs merely because the economic aspects dominate over the legal ones, a situation I would have thought to be true for the whole field of commercial law.

Survey of present valuation method used

The amount of the loan granted to a shipowner will depend on the assessment of ship's value arrived at; the basic security for the loan will probably be a first mortgage on the ship.

The evaluation of ship's value for credit purposes is not necessarily made in the same way everywhere. The main features are, however, not greatly different. An expert will be asked to look into the technical data of the vessel, very much in the same way as described above when explaining the various elements used by brokers and expert valuers to assess the true market value of a ship. The expert or experts will submit a very full description of the vessel and indicate—at any rate outside the UK—ship's value free of commitments, in other words her objective value. The instructions issued by one credit institution will illustrate the point. The seller's value enters as one element in assessing the value. Only the lasting elements of the vessel, it says, and its value to any owner should be taken into account. Values that are of a temporary nature should be disregarded.[1] Commenting on the instructions and the "objective value" a banker points out that whereas the creditor will disregard the particular employment of the ship at a certain moment or during a certain period he will take into account the overall earning capacity of a vessel of that type. In the case of a liner vessel or a vessel used for special transports the knowledge present within the credit institution of that particular market or of the trade for which it is intended will constitute one element in arriving at their assessment of the proper value.

The value arrived at by the experts used by the credit institution will not necessarily be the building costs for the new vessel. These do not automatically represent its value at the time of delivery. The period between signing a building contract and the delivery of the vessel is rarely less than two years, rather more. A new contract for the very same type of vessel signed, for example, on the date of delivery of the vessel ordered, for example, two years ago may very likely, because of rising costs, be much higher than the actual building costs paid; or the development may have gone the other way; owing to a general slump in the freight market or overproduction of that particular type of vessel the contracted price may turn out to be above

1. *Anweisung über die Wertermittlung von Schiffen* by Deutsche Schiffsbeleihungs-Bank AG dated Hamburg 18 August 1969 based on the German Schiffsbank Gesetz of 8 May 1963.

the market price on delivery. This means that actual costs of building will be one but not the only element that has to be taken into account.

The expert valuers are not supposed to look into the way the vessel is chartered if it is the type of vessel likely to sail under charter. The credit institution may nevertheless regard the charter as a general encouragement to grant a credit and perhaps somewhat increase the credit granted. Whether they will regard a favourable charterparty as actually increasing the value of the ship as such or rather adding to the "credit worthiness" of the borrowing party as proof of his skill and talent is hard to say. When dealing with the shipbroker and the price to recommend to his client, be he the buyer or the seller, mention was made that ultimately it was his knowledge, his experience, the "feeling in his little finger" that came as a decisive actor. The same is true for the banker who grants loans using the ship as security. He will take into account all the relevant objective elements. But to that he may well add his knowledge and experience of that particular line, of the owner himself and of the way the vessel is employed. The ship considered as "a going concern" is indeed relevant to him. This would be an outflow of the professional talent commonly ascribed to the banker.[2]

Having obtained the valuation document from the expert valuer and looked into the other elements mentioned above that have a bearing on his estimate of the value to be accepted for credit purposes the banker will grant the loan against first mortgage on the ship and the assignment of the hull and P & I policies. The regular ship's credit institution generally lets the credit run up to one half of "ship's value" only. With shipbuilding prices on the move upwards few shipowners will be able to finance a newbuilding with credit amounting only to 50% of the "objective value". He will have to look elsewhere and point out that as security for a loan his new vessel should be worth much more.

Two Swedish legal writers Tiberg[3] and Grönfors[4] both express their sympathy for the idea that the charterparty should form part of ship's value. It should follow the ship automatically. This would

2. The writer's own recollection from his service on the Board of Directors of the *Swedish Ship's Mortgages Bank* point definitely in the direction that after partaking in the valuation of the experts and all other components that entered the picture a discretionary evaluation of ship's value was made on the basis of the know-how represented within the Board.

3. Tiberg, p. 99 and II, p. 239. Tiberg refers to Braekhus *International Shipbuilding Contracts*, p. 3. See also CMI Conference, Athens 1962, *cf.* below p. 50.

4. Grönfors: *Agande och Brukande*, p. 430.

facilitate the financing of the shipping industry. They are fully aware that this does not represent the legal situation as of today. Grönfors regrets that the law and doctrine do not make it possible to use the value of the ship as a going concern for credit purposes. The legal rules on credit should serve the business world, not hamper its activities. Braekhus points out[5] that whereas granting a loan to a shipowner against a mortgage on his ship is technically a "real property credit" (*realkreditt* is the word he uses), other elements have an important role for the decision of the creditor. He will want to know about the financial strength of the shipowner, his professional skill and his loyalty. They all have a role to play.

The survival of the charterparty in case the ship is sold as a de lega ferenda problem

(i) *The CMI Conference 1962*

The survival of the charterparty in case the vessel is sold was discussed within the CMI in the beginning of the 1960s and was put on the agenda of the Athens Conference in 1962. It was called "*Publicité Naval*" and the angle of approach was that for a third party it would be valuable to know who was the charterer because of the say a charterer had in the running of the ship. A draft convention about registration of the charterparty was prepared, according to which the registration would constitute conclusive evidence of the existence of the charterparty and safeguard its survival in case of voluntary sale, forced sale and probably also in case of bankruptcy. This draft was not adopted.

Grönfors[6] is not surprised that shipowners did not like to have details of their charterparty made public; it would indeed have been difficult, he says, to create registration rules that would prove satisfactory to different types of legislation.

I believe it necessary to be a little more explicit about the discussions at the Conference. The chairman of the working group (the present writer) said in his report to the plenary that both the shipowner and the charterer should be entitled to register all types of charterparties without thereby having to disclose anything but the names of the contracting partners and the duration of the contract.

5. Braekhus: *Kontraktspant i Skip*, p. 304.
6. *Op. cit.*

The registration should constitute conclusive evidence of the knowledge of the contract by third parties and the charterparty would survive the voluntary sale of the vessel. It was suggested that the problem of survival in case of forced sale "should be carefully inquired into with a view to achieving positive results" . . . On Bankruptcy it was felt that this was dangerous ground to walk on and that the subject was hardly ripe for international regulation.[7]

The idea of survival of the charterparty met with little international response. There was no intention of having "details of the charterparty" divulged, as Grönfors says, in the sense that freight rates would be registered. However, the period the vessel was engaged by the charter would have to appear in the register and from this, some said, one would be able to judge the assessment of the market as made by that highly qualified shipowner X and act accordingly. Moreover, shipowners did not want to be tied down even more than at present to a poor charterparty by the registration of it. In such a situation the charterer would look at it differently. And if, on the other hand, the charterparty was advantageous to the shipowner the charterer would not like to become fettered by an official registration of the charterparty. It did not prove to be possible to reconcile these conflicting interests and the project had to be dropped.[8]

(ii) *Discussion within the Swedish Maritime Law Committee and in the Royal Bill to Parliament*[9]

The Swedish Maritime Law Committee discussed the survival of the charterparty at some length and whether rules about its registration should be introduced. The Association of Swedish Bankers and the Swedish Ship's Mortgages Bank wanted this. The Committee came to the conclusion it should not advocate a registration. The problem, they said, had an international bearing. A mere Swedish regulation about registration would have only a limited effect. An international solution was for the time being not to be expected. Unless a voluntary or a forced sale of the vessel was governed by Swedish law registration

7. CMI Conference 1962 Athens. English version of Report, pp. 250/51.

8. Thus if a long term charterparty becomes highly unfavourable to one of the parties (say because the charterparty contains no provision to cope with a currency devaluation) the parties may negotiate and agree about the cancellation of the charterparty against paying damages at a figure to be agreed upon.

9. SOU 1970: 74, p. 136 *et seq.* and Kungl. Majts proposition 1973: 42 *Sjöpanträtt och Skeppshypotek m.m.* pp. 197/201, 293/296.

and inscription under a Swedish statute would not necessarily result in protection for the parties making the charterparty *de jure* attached to the ship. Norway had had up to the present some form of registration of charterparty but the Norwegian Maritime Committee had not the intention of advocating the registration or inscription of charterparty. The Swedish Maritime Law Committee reached the conclusion that it should not come forward with a proposal about registration of the charterparty.

Following Swedish rules the Committee report went to various organizations and bodies for comments. A summary of their views appeared in the Bill that went before Parliament, together with an *exposé de motif* of the attitude taken by the Minister in charge.

Both shipowners and creditors, it was said, are interested in that a vessel can give a regular and good dividend. This makes the ship retain her value and also enables the pledging of the freight as a collateral for credit purposes. The comments on the proposition of the Committee (not to advocate the survival of the charterparty) were widely different. Those who accepted the Committee's view said that an isolated Swedish solution would be of little value to creditors. Those who were opposed stressed the importance of the freight as an object for hypothecation and the weakening of the value of freight as collateral that follows from the absence of legal protection of the charterparty in case of sale of the vessel. A Swedish registration of the charterparty would probably be taken into account abroad, they said.

In the *exposé de motif* the Minister in charge drew attention to the effect for the shipowner of a good and a bad charterparty respectively. The survival of the charterparty if the vessel was sold would increase or reduce the price as the case may be. It could not be taken for granted that a charterer would be prepared automatically to accept a new shipowner. Probably a registered charterparty that survived a sale of the vessel would not look particularly attractive to the charterer. To this should be added the effect of reducing the price that would follow from the survival of a charterparty unfavourable to the shipowner. If such a charterparty was made to survive a forced sale it would make creditors less interested in the protection of the charterparty by legally attaching it to the ship. Moreover, if a special protection of the charterparty was to be introduced into Swedish law it should be a prerequisite that this was recognized and accepted abroad. The international work in this field had met with no success and had been abandoned for the time being.

With all this as a background the Minister in charge did not find it justifiable to introduce a Swedish protection of the charterparty and endorsed the views (not to do so) of the Committee.

Thus we know that neither now nor in the foreseeable future will the charterparty survive the sale of the ship. It is for the new owner and the charterer to arrive at the settlement that suits them best, prolongation or cancellation of the charterer or they may renegotiate the terms of the contract as the case may be.

Evaluation of present situation

I have dealt at some length with the survival of the charterparty as a *de lega ferenda* problem *inter alia* because of the sympathy expressed by the two authors for attaching the charterparty more closely to the ship than today and for their preference for using the *utility value* of the ship for credit purposes.

Has the legal situation as explained a great bearing on the practical situation? Is it a severe handicap to the banking industry that the "utility value" of the ship is not used as a basis for the credit granted? My answer is no. To those credit institutions who follow a cautious policy because of their rules or general approach a *utility value* above the ordinary *market value* of the ship is merely an indication that they do not have to worry, nothing more. In spite of the fall in ship's value during a long depression in shipping some of them have faired well because (i) the original valuation of the ship that they accepted was on the low side, (ii) the percentage of the loan based on that valuation was not extravagant and (iii) they confined their credit engagements to shipping branches with which they were familiar.

Is it a severe handicap to a shipowner that the added value which the *utility value* concept is supposed to give to his ship is not accepted as collateral for credit purposes? Not in the sense that he will fail to obtain elsewhere the additional credit necessary to finance the rising costs of building a new ship.

A study of some of the papers read at the Seatrade Money and Ship's Conferences in 1973 and 1974 go to illustrate that the salient features of financing ships are hardly the assessment of ship's value according to one method or the other. Problems brought to the fore in respect of the long term charters had nothing to do with the survival of the charterparty discussed above.

On the charterparty F W Arnesen[10] said: "Whereas in the old days

10. F W Arnesen: *Banker's view of ship finance*, 1973, p. 17.

. . . there were freight contracts or charterparties and hoop-la [*sic*]
here was the money, the bankers now have to take, and are
increasingly taking a much more flexible view, also evaluating the
risks inherent in a long-time charter or freight agreement". And again
G H Dodsworth[11] who said that the long-term charters had brought
their own problems, increased costs and devalued earnings. "Who in
this room", he continued "who leased a ship five years ago on a ten—or
fifteen—year charter with no escalation is not suffering considerably
today as a result of escalation costs?" So much for the charterparty.
The fundamental issue for credit purposes was pointed out by G A
Newell[12] who drew attention to the three Cs in any textbook on loan
finance: "First cash flow. Where does the money come to repay us?
Collateral: if the cash flow or your primary source of repayment dries
up, what else can you go after in order to keep your shareholders and
depositors happy? Character: Can you believe the answers your
borrower gives you when you are trying to determine whether the
cash flow and collateral are sufficient?" One is left with the overall
impression that the assessment of the borrower is the salient feature in
the financing of ships. Thus P S Douglas[13]: "Banks lend money to
shipowners because they have confidence that shipowners will
generate enough profits to repay their loans. The type of ship
purchased with the borrowed fund is a secondary not a primary
concern of the bank." And again B Quick[14]: "We have several clients
who are very good customers of ours, to whom we will give lines of
credit. We say to them: 'Buy what you want when you want it, then
come and tell us how much it costs' ". Since it is not the purpose of this
study to investigate how and to what extent a shipowner is able to
finance his ship with outside capital, suffice it to say here that the
handicap to the shipowner, if any, of the present situation is not any
difficulty in *finding* the additional credit, rather the *price* he will have
to pay for it.[15]

11. G H Dodsworth: *Package deals and syndicates*, 1973, p. 84.

12. G A Newell: *Financing an expanding fleet*, 1974, p. 106.

13. P S Douglas: *Finance and the future of the supertanker*, 1974, p. 70.

14. B Quick: "Market Conditions and the Availability of money", 1974, p. 103.

15. Where the statutes or by-laws of the credit institutions impose a 50% ceiling
(dating from antiquity, see Grönfors *Ägande och Brukande*, p. 422 and works referred to)
on the credit to be granted the present way of assessing ship's value is obviously more of
a handicap than for those who are prepared to grant loans up to the full purchase price
of the vessel, taking as security not only ship's mortgage but the charterparty duly
assigned. In between these extremes are others like the Swedish State Fund for Small
Tonnage that is empowered to grant credits up to 85% of ship's value using as
collateral not necessarily the first but a second mortgage in that ship or in another. At

That the charterparty does not automatically follow the ship when sold does not strike me as so iniquitous a situation that it should be remedied by a mandatory rule of law. The forced marriage between ship and charterparty has been fully discussed and has been rejected by the parties.

In a situation where you have *on the one hand* high building costs, over-generous credits granted by governmental institutions following official policy rules and/or by private credit institutions lured by the high interest rates obtainable and, *on the other hand*, a substantial tonnage surplus—partly brought about for the very same reasons indicated—a poor freight market is a logical consequence. Where this situation lasts for a very long period it follows that the ship may no longer have a *dividend* or *utility value*. The ship becomes a liability rather than an asset. The creditors are bound to lose money. Many of them have. But the ship may still have an *expectation value*.[16]

---

one time Swedish shipyards were supposed to finance 80% of the contract price for an eight-year period later reduced to 70% and seven years. And there is the situation in Japan where the banks will generally limit their financing to 70% of ship's value but where the largest financing is done by the trading houses that will build the ship in their own name and resell it immediately (at a profit) to the shipowner who has the option of taking all or part of the finance from the trading houses.

These glimpses go to show that *Financing of Ships* is a subject of its own well worth a study devoted to it.

16. What I would call "the Micawber syndrome".

8

Hull Insurance

Hull insurance and certain valuation problems connected with insurance

The English Marine Insurance Act[1] indicates that insurable value of the ship "is her value at the commencement of the risk . . ." The Swedish Marine Insurance Plan[2] (Art. 27) has a general definition of insurable value reading thus:

"the insurable value of the interest insured is, unless such value has not been specifically agreed (assessed insurable value, valuation) or otherwise follows the contract or from the stipulations of this Plan the full monetary value of the interest at any given time while the insurance is in force (open insurable value)".

What constitutes the "value" is not indicated. That is left to the parties to decide. Is this a difficult problem for them? Some say it is,[3] some say it is not.[4]

1. Maritime Insurance Act 1906, s.16(1). *Cf.* "Als Versicherungswert gilt der wert, den das Schiff bei dem Beginne der Versicherung hat". (§ 70 Allgemeine Deutsche Seeversicherungs Bedingungen.)

2. The Scandinavian Insurance Acts are by and large the same. They cover all types of insurance. Denmark and Norway have introduced in their Act a special rule as to the time for assessing ship's value for insurance purposes, this to be her value at the commencement of the risk, natural enough I should say in the days of the voyage insurance. I guess that the traditions from those days proved too hard to overcome in some quarters which goes to explain the difference. It is interesting to note that whereas in the private convention accepted by marine underwriters in Sweden, the Swedish Marine Insurance Plan of 1957, the relevant time is the one indicated in the text. The Danish Marine Insurance Convention of 1934, Art. 9, and the Norwegian Marine Insurance Plan of 1964, Art. 7, both use the commencement of the risk as the relevant time not only for ships but for other subject-matters as well.

3. "Before going any further it must be pointed out that Hull Valuation is a highly contentious subject" (*Notes on Marine Insurance Practice* by Clarus, London 1932, p. 40).

4. G Ripert, p. 2548: "La discussions de la valeur agrée n'offre pas de grandes difficultés dans l'assurance corps. L'assureur connait le navire assuré; il est assez exactement renseigné par les societées de classification; il discute la valeur avec l'assuré et n'agrée qu'une évaluation à peu près exacte. Aussi ne vient-il pas en général après le sinistre discuter l'évaluation de la police."

Selmer, pp. 80–81, speaking generally says, and I agree, that the value to be insured should be the objective value quite apart from any profitable contract that may attach to the subject-matter. The application of this golden principle may not always be easy.

The "valued policy" means that the parties have agreed on ship's value and insured it, in full or in part. The "open policy" means that the parties have agreed on a maximum sum of money to be insured, its exact relation to ship's value to be ascertained when called for by events.

Valued policy. The elements to be taken into account

What are the elements that go into the assessment of the amount to be insured? The owner will want to insure what the ship has cost him to build—or in case of second-hand tonnage the price he has paid. This is a minimum figure. Does that cover the whole ground? Hardly. The contract price entered into with the shipyard may not represent the market value of the vessel when delivered. The time that elapsed between signing the contract and delivery may have brought about a rise in tonnage prices or a fall. In case the prices have gone up the shipowner may feel he must be adequately protected by having his insurance cover the actual market price rather than the amount paid to the yard,[5] or to the seller. The market value and the replacement value are not necessarily the same. The cost of building a similar vessel, to be deliverd in two or three years time may exceed the present market value of the ship to be insured. If the trend has gone the other way the underwriter, at any rate theoretically, may be reluctant to accept the costs of building as the value to be insured in that this may constitute an over insurance and making the owner in theory rather more interested in losing the ship than running it. Cases where vessels are scuttled or cast away do occur. Hull underwriters are aware that the burden of proof with which they are laden makes their position difficult and that they, owing to lack of adequate evidence, are sometimes made to pay for losses that should not properly have been settled. This attitude of theirs has a bearing on the

---

5. ". . . speaking about a British shipping group *The Economist* says 21 July 1973: "They have gone into the charter business on a big scale only recently, and they have tended to fix what they hoped would be safe, long term contracts. But inflation has dealt them a blow, and the in-phrase now is that a shipowner is really a property developer (shipbuilding costs are rising so fast that by the time a ship is delivered it can be worth twice what the shipowner contracted to pay for it.)"

Richter says, p. 855 *et seq.*, that the value to be used for insurance purposes depends on the value of the ship to its owner. The selling value (*Verkauflichkeitswert*) would not be appropriate (*unzweckmässig*), as the assured generally intends to use the ship not to sell it. He would prefer the value for which the ship was acquired or the cost of renewal (*Anschaffungs- u. der Herstellungswert*) less depreciation for wear and tear.

value that they are prepared to accept as an "agreed value". Their professional experience of ship's value will guide them but no doubt also their knowledge of the would-be customer.

Thus the cost to the owner of the vessel is one element.[6] The other is the market value. By and large these figures constitute the minimum and maximum figures and the parties will take them into account when they agree on the proper value to insure for a new building or a recently purchased old ship. When the time has come to renew the insurance of the ship that has had the same owner for one or more periods of insurance the purchase price or the replacement cost may have lost some of its significance in assessing the proper value to be used. The depreciation of the vessel will have much less influence on the value than the state of the freight market.[7] In order to find the proper value to use for insurance purposes the shipowner will look around and compare with values of vessels similar in age and type. He will probably try to get to know how they are insured, a business secret often jealously guarded. Neither when insuring the ship for the first time nor at the renewal of the insurance will the shipowner want to—or rather will he be allowed to—have the vessel insured for less than a figure regarded as satisfactory by the credit institutions that hold the ship's mortgage as security.[8] This will only indicate the minimum figure; the maximum is more difficult to be precise about.

Thus renewal of the hull insurance may well cause as many problems as when the vessel was insured for the first time.[9]

The result of the discussions between the shipowner and his underwriter will to a large extent depend on the costs of insurance. Hull insurance premiums are intended to cover the total loss risk, the cost of repairs and also the third party liability. The third party

6. In the case of *The Orange* 1972 AMC USDC (SDNY), some passages of which have been quoted already, the court made underwriters pay the market value $100,000 in spite of the fact that the assured "had made a fantastic bargain" and only paid $2,800 for the *Orange*, the purchase price not being material fact. There had been, the court said, no misrepresentation.

7. *Cf.* Kofoed and Aagaard Hansen, p. 23 *et seq.*

8. "The bank can never insist on having more cover than the actual loan amount, but in my opinion, no prudent shipowner would insure for less than the market value at the given time". F W Arnesen "Banker's view of ship finance", paper read on 26 March 1973 at Seatrade Money and Ship's Conference.

9. *Cf.* ibid. "As everybody knows the market value does fluctuate widely with supply and demand, and at certain times and for certain ships, shipbrokers have the greatest difficulty in providing price indications which can serve as useful guide lines for shipowners and bankers. It is usually much simpler to decide upon the loan amount when dealing with a newbuilding, because it is easier to establish a fairly accurate market value."

collision risk is in some markets split up between hull underwriters (75%) and P & I underwriters (25%). The value to be insured will influence the premiums asked for. There are, however, other aspects to the premiums than the value that have a say, not easily distinguished from each other. Let me point at some of them. The overall result of hull underwriting in the world market for the last few years is bound to influence premiums in spite of the fact that the formula for calculating the premiums are not the same everywhere. The record of the fleet involved will have to be taken into account. Competition in the market will have a say, so will the cover offered, and the franchise to be used. Thus ship's value is one factor but not the only one that will decide the premium to be paid.

Taking into account the constant rise in the cost of repairs those underwriters who in calculating the premiums make only the total loss proportion of it attach closely to the value insured and calculate the premiums for the cost of repairs and third party risks according to different formulas will insist on having the full value of the vessel covered under the proper hull policy.[10] If too low a figure is insured under full conditions and the top value is covered by some of the other types of insurance, like disbursements referred to below, then the rise in cost of repairs, they will say, coupled with an inadequate value of the vessel covered under the hull policy will make claims for constructive total loss[11] more frequent than if the value insured under the hull policy is made to represent, as nearly as possible, the true value of the ship. They will therefore insist on having the hull policy cover that value. Experience goes to show that the attitude towards insurance of disbursements is not everywhere as restrictive—which may depend on the way premiums are calculated.

Since the first edition of this book (1975) tonnage values have dropped dramatically as illustrated by examples shown in Chapter 3.

---

10. "Ships' values are admittedly on the whole going up but this only affects the total loss premium, which of course is calculated on a percentage of the value. The accident premium is based on ship's size independently of her value. As the agreement about the hull insurance premium is usually made some two–three months before the renewals, and settlement of losses on the average are made some two–three years afterwards, the underwriters carry the whole burden of the inflation": (my translation) P E Hedborg in *Nytt från Assuransföreningen* No. 2 December 1974. This passage is from the first edition. I retain it as an illustration *inter alia* of the fluctuation in ships' values.

11. The problems connected with constructive total loss do not have their proper place in this study, still less so as they were discussed at a Seminar of the Scandinavian Institute of Maritime Law in 1969 introduced by O Steen-Olsen. He formulated his introduction: "The happy shipwreck . . . Something on high agreed hull values and condemnation in marine insurance" (my translation).

Surplus tonnage and drop in the freight market go hand in hand. The shipping industry can no longer generate sufficient capital and is forced to resort more and more to long time creditors. The mortgagers will want to have a say about the amount for which the ship should be insured. In this discussion with the hull underwriters the shipowner will be guided by (i) the purchase price, (ii) the mortgagers' requirements, and (iii) the actual employment of the vessel, perhaps adding a margin on top of the basic value.

Dual valuation

Before looking into different ways besides hull insurance to cover ship's value a word about the dual valuation system has its place here.[12]

We know that the shipping industry is sometimes highly profitable but that there are also periods when it is not. We have been through periods, and for that matter they may come again, when a shipowner could ill afford to cover the full value of his vessel on full conditions. He was able to impose on his hull underwriter the dual valuation system, the low value in the hull policy to be used for purposes of total and/or constructive total loss and the higher one for other ends.[13] The lower value was supposed to represent the market value.

Hull underwriters will look at the market value of the vessel as explained in the careful statistics elaborated by experienced shipbrokers and in technical publications. They will be prepared to

12. Dover, pp. 97, 98 and 301.

13. Writing more than 50 years ago Clarus said, p. 40: "Briefly, this situation can be described as one where there is a serious fall in tonnage values, unaccompanied by any appreciable diminution of the costs of repairs. The disastrous effect of this on underwriting figures can readily be imagined. The premium fund shrinks as the values of vessels shrink, and yet the drain of continual claims still at the high cost of repairs remains unstemmed. It was to cope with this most vital question that the Dual Valuation Clause was drafted, and although in its earlier forms it was not exactly as it appears above, it aimed at the same mark. It must be remembered that a mere maintenance of values on the pre-slump level would not exactly meet the case. The premium would certainly be welcomed by the underwriter, but he would be called upon to pay, in the event of total loss, a sum considerable in excess of the market value of the vessel, and as will become apparent later, the assured might have difficulty in demonstrating a constructive total loss on such a high value". *Cf.* also Tybjerg: *Comments to Danish Maritime Convention*, p. 22. The fluctuations that occur make this passage familiar to situations that happened after it was written and which may come again.

This passage from the 1975 edition shows prescience. Discussions about the renewal of the Dual Valuation System are in the air.

add a certain percentage on top of that value to meet the requirements of the mortgagers.[14]

"We have been very reluctant to dictate to owners what value we think proper for a ship. Instead we adjust premiums accordingly".[15]

Sorting out the market value, the replacement value, the original value, and the credit value, hull underwriters in 1983 tried to formulate their attitude somewhat as follows.

The insurance interest is nearly always more than the value of the thing itself; the market value should be departed from only when there are real factors which call for it; the mortgagee indebtedness should not make hull underwriters accept something that is credit insurance rather than hull insurance.[16]

Hull interest, disbursements

The value to be insured, the cover granted under the policy and the cost of insurance are all three important elements that are taken into account by the parties. For the purpose of this study the total loss risk is the one that is most interesting. Are there other ways more economical to the shipowner to cover it than by hull insurance in the usual way? The way in which the premiums are calculated, of which two methods have been described above, may induce the shipowner to try to insure the top value of the vessel at a lower premium by resorting to types of insurance variously termed as hull interest, freight interest or disbursements.[17]

As indicated already those hull underwriters who make only the total loss proportion of their premium attach closely to the value insured will insist on having ship's full value covered by the hull policy in order adequately to meet the constant rise in cost of repairs.

14. A margin of 10% was indicated to the author by one hull underwriter.

15. S E Svendsen in "Hull Risk Assessment in Norway", paper presented to the Ocean Hull Workshop at the Conference of the International Union or Maritime Underwriters (IUMI) in Tokyo 1985.

16. From the Minutes of the IUMI Conference, Florence, 1983, The Ocean Hull Workshop on the subject "The Valuation of a Vessel—what should be the insurance value?" p. 37.

17. The insurance of freight interest according to the Swedish Insurance Plan (Art. 149) "comprises, whether a contract of affreightment is already concluded or not, the carrier's expected profit on future voyages, to such extent as this interest is not covered by insurance of hull interest or freight or by other insurance".

The disbursement insurance is covered by "Institute TLO Clause (Disbursements)". All three types of insurance are against total loss only.

They will object to shifting a proportion of that value to merely a cover by an insurance of hull interest or disbursements, whereas other hull underwriters who calculate their premiums differently may take up a less negative attitude to having at least part of ship's true value covered by such type of insurance.

When the trade wind blows in the "right" direction, i.e. when shipping is profitable and tonnage prices go up the insurance of disbursements or hull interest mentioned above may well come to the fore. The Swedish Marine Insurance Plan describes insurance of hull interest (Art. 120) as "such interest over and above the insurable full hull value of the vessel that a shipowner has in the preservation of the vessel, to such an extent at this interest is not covered by insurance of freight, freight interest or outfit or other insurance."

The definition of the Swedish Plan indicates that the interest covered by that type of insurance is supposed to be something over and above the market value of the vessel, admittedly a rather vague and nebulous definition. It is not understood in that sense everywhere. In some market insurance of disbursements or hull interest is resorted to in order to cover the actual top value of the vessel.

An insurance of "hull interest" covers, according to the standard insurance provisions used in Scandinavia (unless a wider cover is agreed) total loss only.[18] The borderline between hull insurance on the one hand and freight insurance or freight interest is not always easy to draw. Assuming that a shipowner builds a car and passenger ferry for the line between A and B. The time of building is say two years. The shipowner has a lawful interest to protect during those two years. He may cover that risk by a valued insurance on hull interest. Or to take another example, he may have contracted a ship for five million which on delivery would be worth six million. He may cover the five million under the hull policy and the one million by taking out an insurance of hull interest or alternatively he may cover the six million in his hull policy.[19]

In some markets the proportion of the value that may be covered by insurance of hull interest is limited to a percentage of the agreed value in the hull policy or the hull underwriters must be made aware of such an insurance and, if not, may reduce the amount to be settled for total

---

18. A wider cover than for total loss only is provided for by the "Institute Total Loss and Excess Liabilities Clauses (Disbursements, etc.)".

19. Kofoed and Aagaard-Hansen, p. 111–113; see also G K Schiørring, p. 378.

loss in proportion.[20] Under Norwegian insurance conditions, for instance, the relations between hull insurance and insurance of disbursements or hull interest are made quite clear. That proportion of an insurance of disbursements that exceeds 25% of the agreed value under the hull policy is invalid and payment effected under it and made above the said 25% shall reduce the liability of hull underwriters accordingly.[21]

Insurance of disbursements is thus in some markets regarded as a sort of hull insurance covering total loss only that comes on top of the ordinary hull policy. The limits imposed on the permissible proportion are motivated by hull underwriters' wish to collect the proper premium, their fear of the moral consequences that a high insured value may bring about and the increased risk of their having to meet a constructive total loss because the value of the ship covered under the hull policy is or has become too low.

Selmer[22] points out, and I agree, that while the insurance of "Disbursements Hull" constitutes an addition to the hull policy the underlying economic basis for it is less clear than for the hull insurance itself.

In a rising market the value of cargo liners will probably rise, the values of tankers will rise even more. Thus a tanker that is ready to take on one or several voyages at the skyrocking rates that sometimes are a feature in the market will rise in value accordingly.[23] Whether the owner will cover this

20. P Lureau, p. 136 *et seq.* from which it appears that the French hull insurance policy forbids (Art. 13) insurance "sur bonne arrivée" unless hull underwriters agree. If it is nevertheless taken out they will reduce the amount to be paid for total loss under the hull policy in proportion.

21. Norwegian Insurance Plan Arts. 160 and 223 together with comments. The difficult of drawing a sharp line between hull insurance and hull interest on the one hand and freight interest on the other is illustrated by provision No. 10 in the Norwegian Hull Policy (Cefor form No. 128). If total is covered also by insurance of freight interest, it says, the 25% rule about reduction also applies except where the amount covered by the freight interest insurance does not exceed 50% of the gross freight for the last 18 month period of the remaining time charterparty of charter for consecutive voyage.

22. Selmer, p. 66.

23. The Norwegian Insurance Plan contains a provision (Art. 158) admittedly rarely used in practice, according to which both parties to the insurance contract are entitled to terminate it within a fortnight if ship's value changes materially owing to fluctuations in the market. A P & I Club instruction to its members which I have been allowed to see says: "Members would be expected to ensure that excess liability policies are adjusted as necessary during the currency of the policy in order to conform with any increase in ship's values."

As an *obiter dictum* I should like to add that personally I foresee no future for gold as a unifying or stable element that makes it fit to be used as basis for liability in various international conventions. The solution is rather to resort to the Special Drawing Rights (SDR) of the International Monetary Fund.

additional value to him against total loss only by taking out additional insurance in the shape of "Hull Interest" or "Disbursements" is left to his discretion, subject to the reservation indicated above as to that type of insurance, unless his creditors wish to have a say in the matter.

This paragraph is taken verbatim from the 1975 edition. The "skyrocking rates" sound odd some 10 years afterwards. The long depression in shipping affects both the assured and the underwriter. The shipowner may again—as he did some 30 to 40 years ago—try to arrange his insurance by paying the full risk premium on a reduced value of the ship and the lower premium that goes with the disbursement insurance covering total loss only for the rest of ship's market value. Competition may force the underwriters to comply with the wishes of the assured. Tendencies for using the disbursement insurance in this way are felt in some markets.

In Chapter 12, where I write on limitation of liability I use the vessel *Eve* of 35,000 tons deadweight to show the amount of the limited liability in respect of claims for property damage according to the 1976 Limitation Convention[24] and according to the *fortune de mer* system of the USA. For the shipowner and the claimants it is essential that the amount of the limited liability is adequately covered by insurance. With the tonnage rule system of the 1976 Convention the maximum liability can be fixed beforehand; with the *fortune de mer* system it will depend on ship's value. This should work against any tendency to cover too low a value of the ship.[25]

According to some insurance conditions shipowners' limited liability for claims for property damage will be split between hull and P & I underwriters, or be fully covered by the hull policy. There are other variations as well, depending on the type of insurance taken out. Some aspects of the insurance question I deal with in the section on collision recovery in Chapter 9.

Discrepancy between value insured and value at time of total loss

Scandinavian legal writers have devoted much space to the proper amount to be paid by underwriters where there is a discrepancy between the agreed value insured and the actual value at the time of

24. Convention of Limitation of Liability for Maritime Claims 1976.
25. If and when the shipowner decides to cover only the written down value of the ship as it appears in his books he may not be adequately covered against his third party liability unless a special insurance is taken out in respect of that particular risk.

total loss.[26] For the purpose of this study I do not see that I can add much to what they have said for two reasons. First, under Swedish insurance law an insured value agreed upon stands unless the underwriter can show that the remuneration would materially[27] exceed the amount needed to make good the loss. (Article 30 of the Swedish Insurance Act of 1927.) Thus to challenge successfully a value agreed upon is indeed difficult. Second, my own experience in the profession, and inquiries made with colleagues and with Swedish underwriters show that insured value agreed upon cause few problems in case the vessel is lost. In most cases the amounts agreed upon are paid. The rule laid down in the Insurance Act referred to is intended to protect the underwriter against over-payment and fraud. The influence of fraud has no bearing on this study and I will not take it up.[28]

Two cases will go to illustrate the working of the said provision in the Insurance Act and the view of the court about agreed values.

The *Sea-Gull*,[29] a sailing vessel with auxiliary motor was insured for Kr. 90,000 whereof Kr. 70,000 was to be paid in case of total loss. After a severe fire the vessel was brought to a port of refuge in a poor shape. Official surveyors declared she was not worth repairing and condemned her. The vessel was struck from the official Ship's Register.

Underwriters did not accept the claim for total loss. They said that the *Sea-Gull* was unseaworthy, not properly or fully manned, that the assured had been careless, that there was non-disclosure of material facts at the inception of the risk. If the court did not accept these objections and held them liable they were at any rate not prepared to pay more than Kr. 40,000 which they said was ship's value at the time of the loss.

The Average Adjuster of Stockholm did not accept the objections raised and ordered underwriters to pay in full the 70,000. On appeal, the City Court of Stockholm upheld this decision. In respect of the agreed value the court said: "In the insurance contract the parties have agreed that in case of total loss of the ship payment should be made with Kr. 70,000. Owing to the mandatory character of the provisions in Art. 39: 2 of Insurance Act this

26. F Federspiel, J Hellner, P Hult, U Persson, O Riska in works cited in Bibliography.

27. There are no hard and fast rules as to the understanding of the word "materially". Kofoed and Aagaard-Hansen, p. 27 submit that 10 to 15% is hardly enough even if the amount on which it is calculated, say 20 million will give a substantial figure. Reference is made to *The Dyrstad* case quoted below.

28. Fraudulent action as the only reason that will allow the underwriter to challenge the agreed value dates from Ordonnance de la Marine of 1681 (III-6-23) and is now, owing to provisions in law or in the insurance contracts, the rule in England and Scandinavia and no doubt also elsewhere. Platou, writing in 1900, when this was not yet the situation in Scandinavia, is concerned about the effect of this attitude (Platou, p. 561).

29. ND 1957, p. 579 *et seq*.

agreement cannot prevent the X Company from requesting that the agreed value shall be reduced. As, however, the X Company has not shown that the remuneration to be paid if the agreed value is followed would materially exceed what is necessary to cover the loss suffered by Y owing to the total loss caused by the fire the X Company cannot escape the duty to pay out the amount agreed upon."

Had the court accepted ship's value as being in fact only Kr. 40,000, the court would hardly have made underwriters pay nearly double of that figure. I understand the decision to mean that the difference in values between what the court may have taken as the true value of the vessel and the value for which she was insured was too small to break the agreement on the value in the policy.

In the case of *The Dyrstad*[30] the ship was insured for an agreed value of N. Kr. 75,000. She became a total loss owing to fire. Underwriters were prepared to pay only N. Kr. 25,000 for the loss. The assured insisted on obtaining the full amount agreed upon. The purchase price of the vessel together with investments made in it amounted to some N. Kr. 100,000.

The City Court of Bergen did not accept the views of the assured. The ship was more than 60 years old at the time of the loss. "Ship's strength and value do not increase in proportion to the costs of improvements made. An owner cannot keep his vessel insured for the amount it has cost him if the true value is substantially less.

"The insurance conditions (The Norwegian Insurance Plan of 1940, Art. 16) say that the insurance value is the full amount in money of the subject-matter insured at the time of the inception of the risk . . . The value insured shall not exceed the actual value (*formuesverdi*) of the ship to the owner. When assessing the insured value the market value will generally speaking be decisive. The *Drystad* was not built or equipped for any special trade. The vessel was of the usual freight and fishing type. Similar vessels could be bought. The selling value and the replacement value was about the same. The true insurance value of the *Drystad* is not the cost of newbuilding less depreciation for wear and tear (as submitted subsidiarily by the assured) but what the assured at the relevant time would have had to pay for a replacement of the *Drystad* with a ship of the same size type and age and equipped in the same manner (echo sounding, radio telephone, etc.)

". . . All things considered the court finds that the true insurance value of the *Drystad* in October 1957 was N. Kr. 48,000. The agreed value N. Kr. 75,000 was substantially more than the true value at the inception of the risk. This value" the court goes on to say, "did differ to such an extent from the true insurance value that the agreed value must be held as unreasonable". The court made underwriters pay N. Kr. 48,000.

Thus the court discarded the concept of the cost of newbuilding less depreciation in favour of the replacement value as the true expression

---

30. ND 1960 p. 68.

of ship's value; this value, although agreed, the court thought was manifestly too high and should not be allowed to stand.

The Swedish Hull Insurance Conditions of 1976 go one step further than the Insurance Act and say in so many words that the assessed value is binding on the insurer unless the assured when effecting the insurance gave misleading information about the ship, which was of importance to the insurer when estimating the value of the ship (Art. 2).

This means that in this respect the said conditions follow the pattern existing in France,[31] Norway[32] and the United Kingdom[33] to indicate them in alphabetic order. The cases where the agreed value in the policy is challenged are thus bound to become even less numerous in the future than today.

Unvalued or open policy

When the amount for which the vessel is insured is not a value agreed upon between the parties at the inception of the risk the proper amount to be paid to the assured will have to be decided when a claim for total loss is made. According to the Swedish Marine Insurance Plan one should look to the value when the total loss occurred while under the Danish, English and Norwegian rules already referred to[34] it is the value at the commencement of the risk that counts.

Policies with agreed values are the rule for the ocean going tonnage; not so for the smaller tonnage, the fishing fleet and the yachts. For those categories the use of open or unvalued policies will be much more frequent, for yacht insurance invariably. Thus one underwriter indicated that at the time some 60 to 70% of his 500 hull policies were open policies. Vessels up to 499 tons and fishing vessels were nearly always covered in that way it was said. In spite of the fact that I leave yacht insurance outside the scope of this study there is thus ample reason to devote attention to ship's value in connection with the open or unvalued policy.

"Ship's value" in the case of total loss thus appears in the shape of a claim under the hull policy like the collision claim dealt with

---

31. French Hull Policy, Art. 12 and Lureau, p. 125 *et seq.*

32. The fact that the same rule was introduced in the Norwegian Insurance Plan of 1964 (Art. 8) will help to explain the rule of the said Swedish Conditions.

33. Marine Insurance Act. 1906, No. 27 (3).

34. Danish Convention, Art. 9; English Marine Insurance Act. s.16; Norwegian Insurance Plan, Art. 7.

presently, although the respective claims are not necessarily identical.

In the section on values in general I indicated various models or methods to be used. How far can they be of service when arriving at ship's value in connection with the open policy?

Let us begin by eliminating those that will not assist us.

The *liquidation value* has little to do with ship's value for insurance purposes. Even if it is a single ship company that is liquidated or a calculation made as to what are its net assets, the value of the ship is bound to come up as a separate issue on such an occasion. The liquidation value method will not prove helpful in ascertaining ship's value for insurance purposes. Whether a value computed on the basis of future dividends of the vessel, the *dividend value* method, would give the owner adequate cover in case of total loss is doubtful. The general market for similar tonnage is bound to influence the value of the vessel to be insured. Moreover, it is not easy to ascertain a dividend value for a vessel unless the vessel happens to be regularly employed on a certain trade or committed by a charterparty of some duration. I cannot see either that this method is particularly helpful in connection with the open policy.

Having thus discarded these two methods of calculation we are left with three others, the *market value*, the *replacement value* and the *utility value*.

Let us examine what the Swedish Insurance Act, Art. 37 says on how to make good a loss:

The value of property damaged or destroyed, shall, with the exceptions mentioned in Arts. 38 and 75, be held to be what it would have cost immediately before the event (*försäkringsfallet*) to have the property replaced by new property of the same kind, after deduction of what the property can have lost in value through age, use, reduced usefulness or other circumstances.[35]

How can the five criteria imposed by this Article be made to apply and function when a claim is made under an open policy for the total loss of a ship?

(1) The relevant time for assessing the loss is immediately before it happened. Thus the value at the beginning of the risk does not count,

---

35. Bengtsson 59, Grundt, p. 210 *et seq.* Hellner, *op. cit.* 233/34. St Jørgensen P Lyngsø, p. 146 *et seq.* Sindballe I, p. 134 says: "The insured value of a vessel is not the replacement value immediately before the loss or at any other time but ship's value at the beginning of the risk" (my translation).

nor any fluctuation in prices that may have taken place in the ensuing period until the total loss.

(2) The cost of having the ship replaced by a new ship of the same kind. The wording indicates that one should ascertain what it would cost to build a new ship, unless there is a new sister ship available on the market. (In practice twin sisters hardly exist in respect of ships. There is the difference in age referred to in the section on market value. And technical improvements and alterations are nearly always made in respect of ships built according to the same design.) How will the replacement concept operate while the new ship is built and until she is delivered? A tanker of 200,000 tons deadweight could be built for US $8.5 million in 1967 whereas in the first quarter of 1974 the price was some $24 million. (+185%). Building prices for bulk cargo ships went up in the same period by some 80%. The replacement cost is not necessarily the same as the replacement value. It may cost more to build the ship than what she is worth in the open market when ready. The following example will illustrate the point. If during the second half of 1974 a quotation for building a 200,000-ton tanker could be obtained at all from shipyards the price was probably around $150 per ton deadweight (= $300 million) whereas a four-year-old tanker of 226,635 tons was sold during the first part of January for $23 million, that is to say some $101.50 per ton dw., a fall of more than 32%.[36,37] The replacement cost is no easy yardstick to use when it comes to ships, especially as the period from signing the contract until delivery of the new ship generally is a long one, in spite of improved building methods. The market value of an 85,000 ton deadweight bulk carrier eight years old in 1980 was about $17 million and her newbuilding price some $28 million; the equivalent figures for 1984 being a market value of $6 million and a newbuilding price of some $17 million respectively. In using the US dollar as yardstick we must keep in mind the rise of the rate of

36. The background material for this example has been put at my disposal by L Kihlberg of Kilship AB, Gothenburg.

37. We are getting so inured to inflation at the time when this is written that we forget that this is not the first time that the world has seen production costs rise above the value of the finished product. *Cf Rowan* v. *Clan Malcolm*, a collision in 1921, (1924) 18 Ll.L.Rep 394 *et seq.* where the following passage will illustrate the point. "He (Lord Constable) was not surprised that this difference should have emerged, because the *Rowan* was not of an ordinary type, the re-conditioning which she had received was exceptional, and for the time being general market value had fallen below the cost of construction. In his opinion the consideration last mentioned rendered the method of deducing depreciation from the cost of construction unsatisfactory, although it provided a useful corrective figure."

exchange that has taken place, exemplified above at p. 47 expressed in Sw.Kr. the US dollar was worth 4.39 in January 1981 and 9.02 in January 1985.[38]

(3) What is the proper deduction to be made in respect of a ship for age and use as envisaged by the Act? Some shipowners follow a deduction plan based on annual depreciation calculated on the price actually paid for the ship[39] or the depreciation allowed under the relevant Swedish tax laws[40] whichever is the most favourable in the particular case. Which of them should be taken into account? Should any other model be followed?

(4) How should one apply the words "reduced usefulness"? Is that something more than, or different from, the wear and tear deduction? It might well be. Technical changes adopted for new ships may make another ship outmoded long before its natural span of life has come to an end. Construction prescriptions, raised requirements as to minimum crew, increased wages for the crew may bring about a "reduced usefulness" for a ship that sailed under the flag of the one that became a total loss. Some countries are good at running second-hand tonnage, some are not. What is the proper way to assess that reduction?

(5) One should also take into consideration "other circumstances". What are they? Probably a safety valve to be used when the result obtained using the other four criteria gives a figure that appears unreasonable or unfair.

From what has been said it appears that the provisions of the Insurance Act bring with them too many question marks to be of any great practical help in assessing the proper claim for total loss under an open policy. The variations in the *replacement value*, as shown by the examples quoted here (and also in the section on the time element), also make that method a doubtful test for what hull underwriters should pay under an open policy.[41] It cannot be allowed to be the only one.

38. The figures for 1980 and 1984 are worked out from the graphic analysis of R S Platou, A/S Oslo, put at my disposal by T. Rinman.

39. A depreciation method of 6% per annum up to the first 15 years and then 2% per annum calculated on the price by the shipowner as explained by O Hellberg in *Svensk Sjøfartstidning* 1971 No. 14 p. 24 *et seq.*

40. The Swedish tax provisions allow a tax free deduction in this connection of 20% of the price paid for the ship or 30% of the value with which she appears in shipowner's books.

41. *Cf.* in this connection Nolst Trenité, p. 205 *et seq.* The value to insure should be ship's selling value, not her replacement value as this might cause the assured to make a profit out of the loss of the vessel. Reefers and other specialized vessels represent a

This leaves us with the *market value* and the *utility value*.

The elements that make up the market value of a vessel are explained at some length in the market value section. To use it in this connection is to use the objective[42] value whereas the utility value would represent the subjective[43] approach to the value of the ship. I am not prepared to advocate that one of these models should be applied and the other entirely disregarded. Neither of them can be used as the *sole* test of what the assured under an open policy is entitled to collect from his underwriters. A combination of the market value, the utility value and the replacement value methods had better be resorted to in practice. One should ascertain the value in a free market of vessels of similar size and age, etc., one should attach some importance to the utility value of the vessel lost (for instance the lost fishing boat as the fishing team's only means of gaining its livelihood), and one should look into the figure that would result from the replacement method. The influence of the utility value, if any, will probably push towards a somewhat higher figure than would follow from the application of the two other methods, otherwise the shipowner would not attempt to use it in this connection. The assessment of the value to pay in case of total loss being no exact science one should use the figures so arrived at and see how far they can be made to agree. I submit that in this study, and still less in practice, it is not possible to be more exact on the subject than indicated here.

As against this pragmatic approach it will be objected that to deal with a problem by first looking at the result is not an acceptable way of solving it. One should first take a stand and decide on the method to follow for ascertaining ship's value and having done so apply it in practice. Otherwise the solution arrived at will be unforeseeable and arbitrary. To parry this thrust reference is made to *The Proteus* v. *Cushing* case[44] (cited already when dealing with the time element), where the US Supreme Court said *inter alia*.

It is to be borne in mind that value is the thing to be found and that neither cost of reproduction new, nor that less depreciation, is the measure or sole

higher value to the assured than the mere selling value; that higher value is the one to insure. Due regard should be taken to the type of vessel, her construction, age, condition, market price, etc. It is possible to use the cost for newbuilding and deduct therefrom a certain yearly percentage and in that way arrive at the proper amount to be insured.

42. Drachman-Bentzon and K Christensson I, p. 24.
43. U Persson Op. II, p. 19 *et seq.*
44. 1925 AMC, pp. 779, 783 *Proteus v. Cushing.*

guide. The ascertainment of value is not controlled by artificial rules. It is not a matter of formulas, but there must be reasonable judgment having its basis in a proper consideration of all relevant facts.

This somewhat elaborate analysis of the principle to be followed when settling for total loss under an open policy may give the impression that in practice the problem is a difficult one and subject to much discussion between the parties. Enquiries made in the Swedish insurance market show that this is not so. It is explained that where there is a difference of opinion about the true value of the ship at the time of the loss the opinions of one or two official valuers are asked for or advice sought from abroad. The assessment of the market value will generally be accepted by the parties. If it is not the case is put before the Swedish adjuster and eventually the court.

Perhaps this is too rosy a picture of the true situation. The owner of a vessel insured under an open policy that has become a total loss, with interest earning mortgages to pay is in no strong position to bargain with his underwriters about the value to collect. He may prefer a quick settlement and ready cash to protracted discussions with uncertain results. This may help to explain why Scandinavia has little legal experience of controversies in this field.[45] I have been able to trace two cases that have a bearing, albeit limited, on the settlement to be made under an open policy.

In the first case the points were whether the policy was in fact a valued one or not; in case it was, would the amount indicated if paid give the assured substantially more than was needed to cover his loss.

The *Heddy*, insured for Sw. Kr. 180,000, was condemned. In the adjustment (16 August 1932, Gothenburg) her value in sound condition was indicated as Sw. Kr. 92,000 and underwriters were ordered to pay the said amount. The shipowners appealed. The Gothenburg City Court said (26 February 1943) that . . . "the contract about insurance for an amount of Sw. Kr. 180,000, which had been entered into after a survey arranged by the insurance company does mean that the loss shall be made good according to a fixed value as indicated in the Insurance Act, Art. 39: 2, which being of a mandatory character applies in respect of this insurance contract.

"As against the evidence produced by the assured, Mr I, the Court cannot find that the underwriter U has been able to prove in a satisfactory way that if the said agreement is upheld the allowance of Sw. Kr. 180,000 would be considerably in excess of the amount necessary to cover the loss of the assured owing to the accident. Under those circumstances the agreement is binding on the underwriter U. Out of the said amount the underwriter shall,

---

45. If this study was to embrance also yachts and yacht insurance, which it does not, it is likely that more disputes as to values could be traced than in respect of the merchant fleet. This because open policies are the rule in that branch.

irrespective of the fact that the agreement about the value insured is upheld, pay only 2/3 according to Art. 66: 1 sect. of the Insurance Plan of 1896 or Sw. Kr. 120,000".

The Supreme Court (2 December 1935) said, however: "Even assuming that the insurance contract should be understood to mean that in case of loss it should be made good on the basis of the said value of the *Heddy* the underwriting company U cannot according to Art. 39: 2 of the Insurance Act be bound by such an agreement, which would mean that the amount to be paid out to the assured, Mr I, would according to Art. 66 of the Insurance plan or Sw. Kr. 120,000 be substantially in excess of what is necessary to cover his loss. The Supreme Court therefore finds it right to change the verdict of the City Court and assess the value on the basis of which underwriter U is to pay the loss to Mr I to the amount indicated by the Adjuster or Sw. Kr. 92,000.[46]

The case demonstrates that there may well be a wide discrepancy between what is thought to be the proper value of the vessel at the inception of the risk and at the time of the loss. It also goes to show that it is sometimes open to doubt whether the policy contains an agreed value or is an open policy and that the court was not prepared to let an agreed value stand when, if followed, the remuneration would exceed ship's true value by some 30%.

In the other case three points were raised: Was there a valid claim against underwriters? If so was the policy used an open policy or not? If it was an open policy what was the proper amount to be paid to the assured?

The *Amie* sank. The adjuster said the claim was valid and ordered the underwriters to pay for the loss of the vessel. With respect to the amount to be paid he said:

"As indicated before the *Amie* was insured up to an amount of Sw. Kr. 750,000. According to the insurance conditions of 1966 the amount indicated in the insurance contract is an agreed value (Art. 2) whereas under the special condition in the policy the amount is an open insured value (Art. 6).

"There is thus a discrepancy between the two sets of insurance conditions that apply to the insurance, a discrepancy that has escaped the notice of the parties. If the intention was in effect to make the policy a valued one then the words 'up to an amount of' should have gone out, to be replaced by words like 'agreed value', 'taxed value' or words to that effect. There is thus a lack of clarity which according to general rules should operate against the person who held the pen, in this case the underwriter S; but when one is aware of the fact that the small tonnage is often insured on an open policy and the expression 'up to an amount of' helps to clarify that the intention is an 'open policy' I do not think that in this case there is a lack of clarity that should operate against the hull underwriters.

46. NJA 1935, 13 No. 1049. ND 1935: 449.

An insurance with 'open value' means according to the Insurance Plan of 1957, Art. 27, that the underwriter S has to pay the full value of the ship at the time of the loss.

Two valuation experts have estimated ship's value at the time of the loss at Sw. Kr. 675,000.

This then was the amount the underwriters are ordered to pay."

On appeal to the City Court of Gothenburg the main point, whether underwriters were liable or not was decided in favour of the assured, the Statement was upheld and the insurer ordered to pay the amount of Sw. Kr. 675,000.[47]

The Gothenburg Court of Appeal decided, however, on 24 June 1974 that the assured had no valid claim against hull underwriters. In the circumstances the value of the vessel was not decided on. A request for review by the Supreme Court was made; before this request came up for consideration the case was settled out of court, hull underwriters paying the full amount indicated in the statement, probably a business expedient more than anything else.

I have traced a German case assessing ship's value under an open policy. The *Elisabeth*,[48] insured for Reichmarks 12,000, sank on 13 April 1933 and became a total loss. An expert gave her value at the time as something between Rm 8,500 and Rm 9,500, this being according to him the selling price of similar vessels at the time. The court did not accept the valuation made as it did not have sufficient regard for the fact that the vessel was not an object to be sold but a source of revenue to its owner, and said:

"Diese Schätzungen des Sachverständigen berücksichtigen aber nicht hinreichend den Umstand, dass die *Elisabeth* dem Kläger nicht als Verkaufsgegenstand, sondern in erster Linie als Erwerbsquelle, durch Schiffahrtsbetrieb, diente, und dass der Wert als Verdienstmöglichkeit nicht notwendig identisch ist mit dem auf dem Schiffsmarkte zu erzielenden Verkaufspreise"   .

following which the court fixed ship's value at Rm 10,000. This means the court in this case preferred the *utility value* to ship's *market value*, I am not prepared merely because of this decision to modify my views as to the weight generally to be attached to these methods in connection with the open policy.

47. ND 1973, p. 364.
48. Hans OLG Urt. v. 29.3. 1935—Bf. I 334/35 J R P V 35,271 reproduced under No. 438 in Deutsche Seeversicherung 1923–1957. Sammlung seeversicherungs rechtlicher Entscheidungen nebst Litteraturverzeichnis bearbeitet von J. Sasse, Karlsruhe 1958.

9

Ship's Value as a Claim against Counterparty in Case of Loss Owing to Collision

When there is a collision between two vessels with the result that one of them is lost one of the first questions that will arise is: "Who was liable for the collision?" If both vessels were at fault what proportion of blame attaches to the one and to the other?[1] When that proportion is ascertained, be it by the court or by agreement between the parties, then the parties will come forward with their claim and counterclaim. The owner of the ship that was lost will ask to recover from the other ship the proportion of the loss which corresponds to the degree of liability that attaches to his counterparty. This situation has in principle no particular maritime aspect. It is merely the application in the maritime field of the general law of liability in tort.

Thus ship's value in this context takes the shape of a claim against a third party based on tort. Various methods of assessing ship's value are shown in the general introduction on values. What should be the guidelines to follow? Is there international uniformity in the approach to the problem in respect of collisions claims?

Provisions of law and views of legal writers

The Swedish Act on Damages[2] says:

"In case of damage to property the damages comprise allowance for the value of the property or for the costs of repairs or reduction in value, or for other charges." The Swedish Maritime Code says in respect of collisions (Art. 220) that the party at fault shall make good "the damage and loss that ensues thereby."

---

1. Article 3 of the 1910 Convention on Collision says: "If the collision is caused by the fault of one of the vessels, liability to make good the damage attaches to the one which has committed the fault". This system is not applied everywhere. For a full examination of the apportionment of liability in the various systems of law the reader is referred to Apportionment of Liability, a paper read by F Berlingieri in December 1985 before the Workshop organized at Xiamen—The People's Republic of China—by the Economical and Social Commission for Asia and the Pacific with the assistance of the CMI.
2. Skadeståndslagen (1972: 207). Chapter 5, Art. 4.

Legal writers in Sweden and abroad have addressed themselves to this problem, some of them in a general way and some with ship's collision in mind. Karlgren[3] says that the standard norm should be the interest of the person who has suffered the loss (*quod interest*). This, he says, can cause the damage to become much higher than if tied down to the objective value of the thing lost or its selling/purchase value (the *pretium commune*). Some property may have a much higher value than the mere objective value. Always to use the selling/purchase value may result in too low assessment of the loss. The cost of reproduction is to be preferred without therefore checking whether a replacement takes place or not. The time to be taken into account must not necessarily be the time of the loss; a later date, say the date of the judgment, may well be the relevant date.

To Grönfors[4] it seems most natural to use the term "damage" in the way it is used by the ordinary man that is to say an unfavourable effect for the person who has suffered it. This effect may appear in different shapes. It is difficult to give an overall picture of it but it may be described as the real or actual damage (*realskada*). It will be for the court to say what damages should be paid taking into account the evidence submitted about the utility value, the cost of repairs, the loss of value caused by the damage, etc. The result arrived at by the court may have to take into account the time factor, the local market price, etc. Generally accepted rules established in practice and by legal writers should be followed. I take this last sentence to refer rather to the measure of damages than to a rule on evidence. Hellner[5] is of the opinion that the replacement method indicated in Art. 37 of the Insurance Act should be followed as the main rule also in this connection. The person who has suffered the loss is not bound to accept as damages only the equivalent of the selling value, that is to say the price he would have obtained had the property been sold. Persson[6] by and large appears to be very much on the same lines as Karlgren in this connection.

Speaking of ships the "right to full and complete indemnity" is the expression used by Roscoe.[7] Ameln[8] asserts that compensation for

---

3. Karlgren, p. 142 *et seq.*
4. Grönfors. Trafikskadeansvar, p. 39 *et seq.*
5. Hellner, Skadeståndsrätt, p. 308.
6. Persson: *Skada och värde*, p. 400 *et seq.* also his *Studier*, pp. 1–10, 13–15, 19–26, 34, 41–45, 56–60 convey the same concept.
7. Roscoe, p. 6.
8. Ameln, p. 43.

ship's value causes no problems. One should not feel bound by the agreed value indicated in the hull policy but rather look to the price obtained for vessels similar to the one lost when sold and purchased.

According to J P Govare and J Warot[9] the value to be recovered should be the objective value of the vessel which in practice is difficult to determine. If the vessel lost was comparatively new her replacement value should probably work out to be the reconstruction price, perhaps after some deductions new for old. If the vessel was of a somewhat older date certain rules will have to be followed in ascertaining her value.

The damage shall be measured by the actual value of the ship at the time of the collision Rodière and Lureau[10] say. A new vessel, they say, is probably worth the price for which it was bought whereas with the years its value may have gone down. A favourable market may, however, modify that situation. The value insured is only an indication of the value and the courts should not be satisfied with it as evidence of ship's value. The compensation, according to Rodière and Lureau, should be based on the value when judgment is given, not on the date of the collision. Thus they say if the ship is worth 10,000 at the time of the collision and 15,000 when judgment is delivered the court should award 15,000. Kačic[11] says that the principle of *restituto in integrum* should always be applied in collision cases regardless of the degree of negligence of the wrongdoer.

There is no reason to challenge the principles enunciated above. The *restituto ad integrum* appears to be the generally accepted norm. This will however not prove particularly helpful to the court that has to assess the quantum of damages to be paid. Karlgren and also Rodière and Lureau are inclined to use a later date for measuring the damages to be claimed from the counterparty than the date when loss occurred. The date of the judgment of the court would appear to meet with their approval. The objections raised to this particular point are indicated in Chapter 3 on the time element. A discussion between Scandinavian maritime lawyers took place at a Seminar in Mariehamn in 1976 on the basis of papers presented by *inter alia* K Grönfors and L Rahmn. The subject had already been discussed at the CMI Conference in 1962.[12]

9. J P Govare and J Warot: "La Fixation des dommages intérêts en matière d'abordage en droit français in *Studi in Onore di Giorgio Berlingieri*, Genova 1964.

10. Rodière and Lureau No. 53 and 57, *cf.* above p. 28.

11. Kačic, p. 218 *et seq.* His work is based in part on the preparatory work of the 1962 CMI Conference in Athens.

12. As for further developments see below p. 85.

The CMI Conference 1962

In 1962 at its conference in Athens the CMI dealt with the problem of measure of damages in collision cases. The preparatory documents do not appear in print which is why in some cases I quote from them instead of referring to them.

The resolution adopted by that conference said: "1. The party who has sustained a damage by collision is entitled to be put as far as practicable in the same position pecuniarily as if the injury had not been suffered".

This is a general and unimpeachable wording that can be challenged by nobody, except perhaps from a linguistic point of view.[13] Commenting on the resolution the chairman of the Committee said that some points had been reserved for further studies ". . . in the first place the assessment of the quantum of damages, such as the valuation of a ship when lost and the cost of repairing a ship when damaged."[14]

Some passages from the preparatory works illustrate the views entertained on ship's value in this connection.

According to English law and practice, the British Maritime Law Association said[15] the owner of the vessel lost is entitled to recover its market value. If the vessel is of a special character or is engaged in a special trade the market value is deemed equal to the value of the vessel to the owner as a going concern. If the vessel at the time is engaged under a profitable charterparty this fact should be taken into account. The present value of the future earnings of the charterparty should be included in the value of the vessel, subject of course to no special claim being made in that respect.

The use of the expression "the value of the vessel to the owner as a going concern" is tantamount to saying the value of the vessel with commitments discussed at some length in the part above devoted to the valuation system in England.

It is interesting to compare this view with others that were put to

13. CMI Procès Verbaux Conférence d'Athens, 1962, p. 277. The French version sounds like the original: "La réparation doit mettre la victime dans une situation aussi proche que possible de celle qui eut été la sienne si l'abordage ne s'était pas produit" (1 d, p. 276).

14. CMI English version of Conference Report, p. 247.

15. $\dfrac{\text{Dom. 15}}{3\text{–}59}$ = the way the CMI designated the various replies submitted.

the Conference. Thus the Maritime Association of the Federal Republic of Germany said:

In case of total loss the proper value of the ship at the time of the collision is to be compensated. The proper value of the ship is her value if sold in the international market. If, however, the sale of the ship is restricted by national legislation this is to be taken into account. Compensation is due for the material value of the ship only and not for any goodwill which may attach to the ship as a unit of her owner's fleet. Quite apart from this stands the question of loss of profit which will be dealt with under item IV.[16]

The Swedish reply makes the same distinction between ship's value and loss of profit.[17]

Damage to the ship herself should be based on the costs of repairs or, in the case of total loss, on the value of the vessel at the time of the collision, the value being an assessed value based on the open world market.[18]

The additional loss the owner has suffered as a result of the collision—e.g. the freight for the voyage during which the collision occurred; anticipated losses on future fixtures already entered into; loss of business to a liner owner unable to maintain his advertised schedule; and of course detention during repairs.

The distinction between the two set of claims,[19] the value of the ship and the loss of earning is observed less clearly in the Norwegian reply.[20]

In accordance with the general principle mentioned before it is the *individual loss* which is to be compensated. If, therefore, the vessel is totally lost, the court must determine the value of the particular vessel to the particular owner . . . The market value in practice is often resorted to as a means of ascertaining the loss, and if no particular interests attach to the vessel over and above the market value this amount will be awarded. But the market value is not used as a means of "normalizing" the compensation. Any loss on top of the market value must be compensated.

---

16. Reply of German Maritime Law Association to Questionnaire under point III. The document (not in print) is designated by the CMI as $\frac{\text{Dom. } 17}{7-59}$.

17. Reply of Swedish Association of International Maritime Law $\frac{\text{Dom. } 3}{2-58}$.

18. As to the market value being used *cf.* for the USA *The Blanche C Pendleton*, already referred to (1924 AMC 382 4 CCA ED Va) where the measure of damages for the sinking of a vessel by a collision was taken as the market value at the time of the collision, not the replacement value.

19. This distinction appears to be true elsewhere. *Cf.* Belgian law where, according to Jacob, p. 518, the owner in case of total loss is entitled to recover from counterparty (a) the value of the vessel as decided by the judge *ex aequo et bono*, less proceeds if any (b) the loss of freight and (c) damages for delay.

20. Dom. 4. Reply of Norwegian Association of Maritime Law.

In order to cover the loss of earnings until a new vessel can be procured, or the compensation otherwise invested, it is not unusual to award the market value plus a certain "interest" on the market value for a certain period of time (ND. 1939.148; 1939.360) . . .

A good charterparty or a bad charterparty attaching to the vessel at the time of the total loss affect the market value of the ship. It is reasonable to believe that the court will award compensation in accordance with the market value . . .

In the USA the owner is not entitled to recover loss of earnings for a total loss in a collision case. "The damages are limited to the value of the vessel with interest thereon and the net freight pending at the time of the collision."[21,22]

Ship's value and loss of profit

I believe it is necessary at this stage to come to grips with the two elements that are to a certain extent mixed up with each other in the quotations and references indicated above, on the one hand ship's value, on the other the loss of profit. It is also necessary to show some of the consequences that follows from the English method of assessing ship's value "with commitments".[23]

The difference between the ship's value and loss of profit becomes clearer if the collision does not bring about the total loss of the vessel. If damage sustained takes three months to repair the claim against the counterparty will consist of two items, the repair bill and the loss

21. *The Umbria* 166 US 404 (1897).

22. At the CMI Conference in Lisbon 1985 the delegates from the UK and the USA pointed out that their courts did not normally permit separate claim for loss of use of the sunken vessel as the loss was already included in assessing the value of the vessel. Is the use of the word "normally" an indication of a possible alignment with the civil law countries?

23. It is interesting to note that in 1939 the Norwegian writer J Jantzen (*Erstatning for frakttap ved forlis som en følge av sammanstøt*, ND 1939, p. 417 *et seq.* upheld the distinction between the claim for ship's value on the one hand and the loss of freight on the other. Not so the Danish writer C Marcussen in a lecture delivered before Forsikrings-foreningens Søforsikringsgruppe in 1956 (the manuscript of this lecture has kindly been put at my disposal by the author; a resumé of it appears in Assurandøren No. 13/14, March 1956 in Dansk Forsikringstidende No. 14 of April 1956). He expressed the view that in a collision claim ship's value should be assessed in such a way that the shipowner did recover the extra value the ship had to him because she was specially built or particularly suited for the trade where she was employed or such extra that may derive from her profitable commitments; whereas the poor charterparty should not, he said, be made to reduce the claim for the ship lost below ship's ordinary market value.

For reasons that will appear in the text I do not agree with my colleague Mr Marcussen.

owing to the immobilizing of the ship for three months. This latter claim, commonly referred to as the "demurrage"[24] claim, will be made up of (i) ship's running costs in the period she is out of service owing to the collision and (ii) the loss of profit sustained. What should go into the one and the other category will generally be the result of deliberations, sometimes long and difficult, between the parties.[25] The ultimate beneficiary of the recovery in respect of items (i) and (ii) should in principle be the shipowner himself.

The recovery obtained from the counterparty for the items eventually agreed upon will be distributed between hull underwriters and the shipowner. Hull underwriters will take the proportion that attaches to the cost of repairs he has paid, the balance being for the shipowner himself and/or for the loss of hire underwriters, if any, that may have paid him for part of the time the ship was immobilized. When the claim against the counterparty is for total loss I submit the same distinction should be upheld as in the example quoted, that is to say ship's value on one side and the claim in respect of time and loss of profit on the other.

If the court decides that damages for the ship lost should include the increased value that follows for her profitable commitments being taken into account it would follow that the loss of profit element, the *lucrum cessans*, is taken care of as well. In principle the value of the ship free of commitments together with a separate item for loss of profit should produce the same amount of damages. Whether an English court would reduce the compensation because the ship was committed to a non-remunerative charterparty is still an open question. No doubt it would be logical to do so but I very much doubt if pure logic would be allowed to prevail to that extent in a collision case.

Effect on distribution of recovery

How does the method of evaluation of the vessel work out on what I term the receiving end in case of total loss? As in the case of partial loss

24. "Demurrage" used as a term to express time lost in collision cases is demurred to by some. It should properly be reserved to the additional days paid for by the charterer at a fixed rate. Some support for the practitioners' lax use of "demurrage" in describing the period of time lost owing to a collision may be derived from the explanation given by Carver, para. 1812, p. 1259.

25. The subject of compensation for damages in collision cases is at present (1985/1986) examined by the CMI. Only such aspects of the problem that affect ship's value will be discussed in this study.

described above, hull underwriters that have settled for the total loss of the vessel will be entitled to the proportion of the recovery that attaches to ship's value which reflects the amount they have settled. If a recovery is obtained for loss of earnings this will go to the shipowner or to the set of underwriters that have covered that risk.

If an English court decides that damages should be paid on the basis of ship's value with commitments, say value of free ship 15,000 plus the value of her commitments 5,000 = 20,000. Hull underwriters will collect the amount they have paid or 15,000 for total loss under the hull policy. Where will the balance, the 5,000, go? Will the charterer claim them and if so will he succeed? Will the charterer, in support of a claim for the 5,000 say, for instance, that he has financed the building or the purchase of the ship lost, that he has entered into a long term charterparty that has proved highly profitable to the shipowner, that he, the charterer, in all but a nominal way is the owner of the ship that was sunk and that logic would have it that the added value of the ship that the English court has ascribed to it is the result of the benefit his contract gives to the shipowner and should be his? For all I know the charterer may try to obtain the 5,000 on the basis of these or other arguments but I cannot see how he could succeed.[26] The "subjective value", with commitments, used by the English court represents the value of the ship to its owner. The value above the market value, the 5,000 in the example, is the capitalized value of shipowners' loss of profit and should in principle go to him.

If the shipowner has taken out additional insurance say for "hull interest" or "disbursements hull" or "loss of freight" or "freight interest" it will depend on the terms of the insurance conditions if and to what extent that particular set of underwriters will be entitled to the 5,000 used in the example. The terms are not necessarily the same everywhere in this respect. As an example I quote from the Swedish Insurance Plan, Art. 124, about the right of recovery accorded to underwriters of hull interest:

Such share (in the recovery) is, however, only due to him out of the part of the

---

26. Whether the time charterer has a right of direct action against the other ship in a collision is a problem of its own. It has been investigated on a comparative basis by Dr H C Albrecht of Hamburg in a stencil dated 30 July 1973 which I have had the privilege of seeing. For this study devoted to ship's value I believe it is enough to say this: If an English court should rule that a shipowner obtain from the counterparty an amount that is below the ship's market value (admittedly an unlikely situation in spite of its logic) because the ship was committed to a low rate charterparty of some duration then the tortfeasor would derive a benefit at the expense of the time charterer and the time charterer should in my view have a right of direct action against the other ship.

said allowance or the net recovery that remains after the share applicable to the insurable value for full hull has been set aside and to such an extent as the allowance or the recovery has been received in respect of loss which the insurance of hull interest was intended to cover.

How does the amalgamation of the objective value of the ship with the profit element described as the "value of the vessel to the owner as a going concern" into one figure work out when the counterparty is not 100% liable (incidentally a most unusual situation) but to a lesser degree, say 80%? The amount recovered in the above example would then be 80% of 20,000 or 16,000. This is more than the total loss amount settled by hull underwriters. Are they entitled to the 15,000 they have paid leaving 1,000 to the other interest? Do they collect only 80% of the agreed value under the hull policy 15,000 or 12,000 leaving 4,000 to the other interests? This is no treatise on insurance problems and rights of subrogation. I will not try to solve this or similar problems here. They are brought in merely to show the complexity that follows from the concept that ship's value in collision cases should be made to include a profit element. The profit in my view had much better be shown as a separate element.

Evaluation of English method of valuation in connection with collision claim

The foregoing shows that to me the measure of damages in collision cases where ship's value is taken as her "subjective value," her value "to the owner as a going concern" has little appeal if any. It means putting together under one and the same heading the objective value of the ship, as it may appear from her general market value, with the loss of profit that may be due to the owner because of the loss of his ship. Lack of logic is, however, something to which the business world probably can adapt itself. The practical consequences of the English concept are less acceptable. The distribution of the recovery obtained becomes more difficult, as illustrated above, when on an essential point there is confusion as to for whom the banknotes are earmarked, the hull underwriters, the shipowner himself, or the underwriters of the profit element, however described. This aspect I sum up in the words "Fusion causes confusion". The English method is not necessary to give the claimant adequate protection for his loss. He will obtain that as well outside English jurisdiction where the profit element is dealt with as a separate item. Moreover, the English method in collision cases has unfortunate repercussions in salvage cases, as will be explained presently. Finally, is not international uniformity desirable, especially where it can be made to operate without harm to the interests the English courts want to protect, the shipowner who has lost his ship?

Application of methods of valuation

Which, if any, of the valuation methods described in the section on values in general can be used in assessing ship's value in a particular context, here as part of a claim for collision damages.

It is easy to see why the *liquidation value* will not prove helpful in this connection. Nor does the *dividend value*, defined already as the present discounted value of the future stream of income, have its proper place here. It comes too close to the subjective value with its inbred profit element to which I have taken exception above.

If a ship similar to the one lost is to be found in the international market the *market value* can be used, subject to adjustment for discrepancy in age, etc. If the ship that went down had a special usefulness for the owner because she was well adapted for the special trade where she was used and such a ship can be found in the market then it should be possible to take into account the additional price such owner may be inclined to pay for it; in other words the *utility value* might be accepted. Where the market value cannot be used because there is none either because of regulation from public authorities or because the vessel is of a too specialized type to appear on the market one is left with the *replacement value* favoured by Hellner (*vide supra*) that is to say "the cost of a new similar property after deduction for wear and tear". To make that method function well in connection with the replacement of a ship is not easy but probably feasible. The time of delivery of a new ship, the increased contract price, the sliding scale, or the fall in prices owing to overproduction, the fixing of the proper yearly depreciation for the ship lost compared with the replacement ship, the technical improvements that are likely to have taken place and to boil this down into a figure that will prove acceptable to the counterparty will indeed be difficult. However, it may have to be resorted to when there is no other method that can be made to apply. That is to say when the search for the market value, determined by comparison with contemporaneous sales of similar vessels, has proved definitely fruitless.

It is possible to foresee situations where none of the three methods described constitute the only choice open in assessing ship's value in a collision claim.[27] Ships may be on the market that have much in common with the ship lost although not exactly similar. Vessels may be available that subject to modification can be used by the owner in the particular trade where he used to operate his ship. Their respective utility value can somehow be made to compare. It may perhaps be possible to weave together the different elements that together make up the replacement value as indicated above. An arbitrator, or for that matter the court, might care to know, subject to the reservation explained, that the market value was 10,000, the utility value 15,000 and the replacement value 17,000. What would be the sum the counterparty would be made to pay? The award would not be less than the bottom value 10,000 nor more than the top value 17,000. The arbitrator or the court may not be tainted by the adjuster's professional inclination towards the arithmetic median when estimates as to ship's value differ and adjudicate 14,500. Or may they? This said, we are as near to a probable solution to the problem as we may safely get in a study of this kind.

The situation within the CMI in 1985

The measure of damages in collision cases is again on the agenda of

27. The difficulty of implementing one single method is illustrated in case of *The Saivo* v. *Windward Island* (ND 1959, p. 445 *et seq.*). The *Saivo* became a total loss after the collision. Her owners claimed her value of Kr. 8,250,000 from the counterparty. In arriving at that figure they had not, they said, taken into account the special value that the vessel represented to them because of her speed, characteristics and use. The loss of freight was dealt with as a separate item. The counterparty was prepared to accept a value of some £460,000 to £470,000 for the *Saivo* (representing in Swedish money in round figures Kr. 6,600,00, at the time).

The Stockholm City Court (the case went no further) said it was difficult to assess ship's value on the basis of prices obtained for similar vessels as no vessels directly comparable to the *Saivo* were sold at the time. The nearest comparable one was the *Dagfred*. She was, however, five years younger than the *Saivo* and was a combined tramp and liner vessel that made her particularly attractive in the market. The *Dagfred* was sold in a steeply rising market and the price obtained for her was presumably a good one indeed.

The court took into consideration on the one hand that the *Saivo* was well built, that she was specially reinforced, that she was in good upkeep at the time of the loss and on the other that she had been used for 11 years in strenuous transports of ore. Taking all this into account the City Court assessed her value at the time of the collision as Kr. 7,250,000.

I read the *Saivo* to mean that the court attached importance to ship's market value, but that it was hard to say for certain what it represented at the time, that other elements taken into account were the extra value that resulted from ship's construction and her good upkeep as against which the court set the extra depreciation warranted by the exacting trade where the *Saivo* had been employed for quite some time.

the CMI in 1985. The intention is to produce guidelines generally acceptable and accepted on the model of the York/Antwerp Rules.

In 1985, a Working Group within the CMI produced a draft of which the part dealing with total loss reads as follows:

Rule I—Total Loss
(i) This Rule applies to a vessel which, as the result of a collision, is an actual total loss and to a vessel which is damaged to the extent that it is not economically justifiable to have it repaired.
(ii) Damages recoverable shall include the value of the vessel; such value shall be the value which it represented to its owner, account having been taken of the type, age, condition and nature of operation of the vessel at the time of the collision.
(iii) Where, however, it is possible to acquire a similar vessel, the value of the vessel shall be determined by reference to the cost of acquiring such similar vessel.
(iv) Damages recoverable in the event of a total loss shall also include:
  (a) compensation for the loss of use of the vessel for the period reasonable and necessary to find a replacement whether the vessel is actually replaced or not. Such compensation to be calculated in accordance with Rule II (iii).

No final decision about the guidelines has yet been taken by the CMI (March 1986).

I O

Salvage

The Salvage Convention[1] indicates in Art. 8 under (a) the factors that have to be taken into account first when fixing the salvage remuneration, such as the success obtained, the danger run, the time expended, the expenses incurred, etc., and under (b) as a secondary factor, the value of the property salved.

The Pragmatic approach

Salvage being a subject where the adjuster, albeit only as a spectator, is bound to pick up some practical experience I had better use it and take a pragmatical approach to the subject.

Salvors are interested in the value of the property salved, but not overmuch, provided they feel satisfied that the value is sufficient and adequate to cover a proper remuneration for their salvage services. The value of the cargo I leave aside. It has no place in this study. If ship's value in sound condition is somewhere around one million pounds or more salvors will know values are sufficient to meet any reasonable claim. They will then not be particularly interested in the exact value and how it is calculated.[2] To avoid difficulties about values, shipowners in Sweden or rather their hull underwriters, will ask an official valuer to give his view on the sound value of the vessel at the time and place where she is brought by the salvors. They will ask the valuer to indicate the general market price of the vessel free of commitments, as explained above in the section on market value.

If ship's value is below the figure of one million pounds experience shows that salvors become more interested in her value. They have learned over the years that what they think is adequate remuneration is more difficult to obtain if it works out as a high percentage of the

1. Convention for the unification of certain rules of law relating to assistance and salvage at sea, Brussels 23 September 1910.

2. "The exact or precise value of the salved property, particularly when that value is high, is not essential in order for a salvage award to be made." Norris/Benedict, Vol. 3A, §260 (the work of Norris having been incorporated in Benedict 7th edn.).

value of the property salved. In this situation different valuers may be consulted, one by salvors, one by those acting for the ship salved, i.e. the shipowners or their hull underwriters or more than one valuation expert from each side; the values indicated will be compared and more often than not a compromise as to ship's value will be arrived at.

Importance to be attributed to salved values[3]

What importance should be attached to the value of the property salved belongs strictly speaking to the law of salvage rather than to a study on ship's value. To investigate that aspect of ship's value unless it had an important impact on the salvage remuneration would, however, be somewhat frustrating. The following will show that it is well worth examining the subject.

Schimmering says that the salved values should not be allowed to influence the remuneration due to salvors. He is however aware that in practice this is not so and that the values play a great role especially when they happen to be considerable.[4] That is probably the point.

The Bytom case[5] the City Court of Gothenburg said that considerable weight should be given to the fact that the value of the property salved was important. That the values were important indeed, the Gothenburg Court of Appeal said, had the effect of materially increasing the amount of the salvage remuneration. This decision was upheld by the Supreme Court.[6] This attitude is in no way unique. The Maritime Arbitration Commision (MAC) of the USSR Chamber of Commerce and Industry said:

Taking into consideration the success of the salvation, the work and the services of the salvors, the danger to the salved and the salvaging vessels as well as the time spent and *the high value of the salved property* . . .''[7] (my italics) and again "taking into account the success of the salvage, the danger to the salved ship and her cargo, the degree of the salvage operations the expenses made as well as *the importance of the value of the salved property* . . .''[8] (my italics)

3. For the entire problems in arriving at the proper salvage remuneration reference is made to the paper read by J Schultz on the occasion indicated above in fn. 1, p. 75.

4. Schimmering, p. 32 *cf.* Kennedy, p. 183. Schimmering's assertion is of course not correct. See Art. 8*b* of the 1910 Salvage Convention.

5. NJA 1955 p. 386 *et seq.* ND 1955, p. 254 *et seq.*

6. Juglart and Villenau, p. 307, commenting on *The Bytom* case say: "L'importance des valeurs sauvées donc un facteur determinant dans la fixation de la rémunération".

7. *The Rafael*; Award 21 December 1970 in *The Baltic Shipping Co and the Latvian Shipping Co* v. *The Novorossijsk Shipping Co* reproduced in "From the Practice of the Maritime Arbitration Commission" (1969–1971), p. 22 *et seq.*

8. *The Merkantas*: Award 20 May 1971 *The Latvian Shipping Co* v. *the Co "Mercandia"*, *Copenhagen*; reproduced in "From the Practice of the Maritime Arbitration Commission" (1969–1971), p. 26 *et seq.*

The salved property, Norris/Benedict say,[9] in one of the factors to be considered. Large valuations frequently result in more liberal awards but the award does not rise proportionally with the rise of value.

I understand Braekhus[10] to mean that when the value of the property salved is particularly important the salvage remuneration will have to be assessed at a lower percentage than would follow from a mere percentage rule, whereas, when the values happen to be very low the percentage will have to be increased. He quotes *The Queen Elizabeth* (1949) 82 Ll.L.Rep 803, where Wilmer J said that one cannot:

measure salvage awards as sums in arithmetical proportion in relation to the salved property when you have values of the magnitude that you have in this case, but equally it would not, I think, be right to say that, where you have a value of this size, the addition of a few millions or the substraction of a few millions would make no difference whatsoever. So long as even an outside chance of anything in the nature of total loss remains, then I think that the increase of value must involve some, although possibly not great, increase in the salved award over and above what might have been awarded had the value been much smaller.

Ship's value after salvage, the pragmatic approach

When a vessel needs salvage assistance she is obviously in distress. Something has happened to her or to the cargo on board. When brought in safely to port by the salvors she is more often than not in a damaged condition. Repairs may be carried out at the place of refuge where the salvors brought her or she may have to proceed, under her own power or with assistance or escort, to a port of repair. The salved value in the sense of the Convention is obviously not her value in sound condition as assessed by the expert valuers referred to. From this value will have to be deducted the cost of repairs and also the necessary cost of removal to a port of repair as the case may be.

The place where the salvage services come to an end will be *the* place that counts for assessing the value of the vessel for salvage purposes.

The case of *The Remøy*[11] will illustrate some of the factors that have to be taken into account for assessing ship's value.

9. Norris/Benedict Vol. 3 A, § 258 (the work of Norris having been incorporated in Benedict 7th edn.).
10. Braekhus, p. 81.
11. ND 1982, p. 204.

Some of the points raised came before Frostating Lagmansret (Norwegian Court of Appeal) in 1982 in the case of *The Remøy*. The *Remøy*, a trawler built in 1965 and rebuilt in 1976, grounded on the coast of Labrador in November 1978. The trawler *Arctic* managed to refloat her and towed the vessel to Bonaventure, Newfoundland. A tug towed her to St John's. Hull underwriters made a salvage vessel bring the *Remøy* back to Norway. Extensive repairs were effected and the vessel was then sold. In the dispute about the salvage remuneration due to the *Arctic* the owner of the *Remøy* took the position that the vessel had practically no value in damaged condition at ·Bonaventure. To facillitate the understanding of the decision of the court the following figures are indicated in US dollars, converted from Norwegian Kroner and presented in round figures.

The *Remøy* was insured for $4,050,000, the actual cost of repairs was $3,643,000, the price obtained at the sale of the completion of repairs was $3,240,000. The rough estimate of cost of repairs made in Canada was $2,430,000. Repairing ship's bottom damage, only inspected by divers in Canda, would probably cost some $810,000. Hull underwriters intimated (letter of 30 January 1979) that a prospective buyer was prepared to pay between $565,000 and $648,000 for the *Remøy* in St. John's and later (letter of 6 August 1979), that according to them the *Remøy* was worth about $1,050,000 in Bonaventure. The value of the crayfish catch on board, $393,000, was not in dispute. How did Frostating Lagmansret deal with this wealth of figures?

It was difficult to assess the market value of the *Remøy* in damaged condition at Bonaventure, the court said. The assessment of the cost of repairs made in Canada was probably too optimistic. The ship's bottom was only inspected by divers. The cost of the ultimate repairs and the price obtained for the *Remøy* after they were completed were both elements to take into account when assessing the salvage remuneration. The owner's contention that because the cost of repairs exceeded the sale's proceeds obtained the *Remøy* had no value at Bonaventure the court did not accept. The court expressed doubts as to whether the price obtained for the *Remøy* when sold was in fact the best price obtainable for a newly repaired vessel, the buyer had probably made a good bargain. The market value of the *Remøy* before the grounding was probably around the figure for which she was insured. The estimate of cost of repairs made in Canada, together with the submission of one of the experts about the probable cost of repairs of ship's bottom damage would give a figure of $810,000. The court was not prepared to form an opinion on whether insured value, less estimated cost of repairs, was at the same time the actual and obtainable market price. The price of trawlers like the *Remøy* depended to a large extent on the prospects of obtaining a licence for crayfish trawling. Rebutting the submission that the *Remøy* had only a negative value at Bonaventure the court drew attention to the fact that hull underwriters decided to have her towed back to Norway for repairs. The prices indicated by the hull underwriters in a letter of 30 January 1979 as obtainable in St John's and their own estimate of ship's value at Bonaventure all spoke against the shipowner's submission that the *Remøy* had a negative value at Bonaventure.

The final ruling of the court as to the salved vessel with her catch was \$1,202,000—and the salvage remuneration, confirming the ruling of the court below, was \$972,000. This means that the value of the *Remøy* was assessed by the court at \$809,000 (=\$1,202,000 less value of ship's catch \$393,000).

What a prospective buyer would pay for a vessel in damaged condition lying at a place where she cannot be repaired and whence she can practically not be removed will depend on the particular circumstances at hand. The seller will insist on obtaining at least her scrap value at such place. But what is her scrap value in the situation described? Can she be moved to a breaking up yard. Can she be broken up entirely or in parts, where she lies? Will the harbour authorities step in and force her to be removed or destroyed? In other words, does the ship in the hands of her owners (or hull underwriters that have settled for total loss) still represent an asset or a mere liability? These elements many enter into the hard bargaining that will ensue with prospective buyers. The writer can remember a case where, owing to the local condition in the country X, no buyer dared to come forward with a bid for a small vessel because coastal traffic was then the monopoly of the President of that country. It is probably true to say that whatever the political situation it is more likely that the prospective buyer will make a good bargain than the seller. A similar situation that works out to the detriment of a seller and upsets the effect of a free market when assessing ship's value for salvage purposes may be brought about by public authorities fixing ceiling prices for ships or restricting their sale. I have discussed this situation under the section on market value.[12]

12. Thorbjørnsen, p. 277 *et seq.* gives an incisive analysis of the situation in Norway when a ceiling price for tonnage was introduced making sales above the price existent on 8 April 1940 (the day before the German occupation of Norway) unlawful. This regulation remained in force throughout the war and for some years thereafter with the effect as already mentioned that practically no sales took place at all. When no ships are bought or sold the term "market value" has no sense. *Cf.* above p. 31.

Repairs, the time element

To assess ship's value when salvage operations are terminated the amount of the repair bill or the estimate of experts will have to be deducted from her sound value.

Sometimes the repair period will be a long one, waiting for engine spare parts, etc., and the ship will lie idle. Should this time be taken into account in assessing ship's value?

A prospective buyer will be aware that he cannot use the vessel for commercial purposes for quite some time and he will ask for a reduction in price. Thus time has a price in this connection. A reduction of the salved value of the ship owing to a protracted period of repairs has found favour with Lloyd's arbitrators in a number of cases.

How to assess the value of salved ships

What has been said gives some idea on how the value of the vessel for salvage purposes is arrived at and will serve as a background for legal writers that have dealt with the subject.

Norris/Benedict[13] enumerates seven methods that can be used to that end. The value by stipulation, that is to say that the partners agree on the value, is the most frequently used he says.[14] This is in full accordance with what is said at the beginning of this section. Ship's value when new less yearly depreciation is the method that can be used "where there has been no appreciable change in her value from the time of her construction", no doubt a substantial reservation. The third method "after repairs" means either ship's value after repairs or ship's "original value" less depreciation and cost of repairs. What does the "original value" mean here? The price obtained at the sale of the vessel pursuant to court orders will be accepted he submits.[15] Ship's value appraised by experts appointed by the court are open to accordance or rejection by the court. The market value is, however,

---

13. Benedict, incorporating Norris, Vol. 3A, §§ 262/263.

14. *The Songa* ND 1978, p. 164; *A Cabin Cruiser* ND 1979, p. 325

15. This is I think too definite an assertion. In *The Lyrna* [1978] 2 Lloyd's Rep 27 the salvage operation ended on 9 December 1976. The vessel was sold by court action in June 1977 for £32,000. It was argued before Brandon J that any sales of court had the character of a forced sale with the result that the amount obtained was likely to be appreciably less than in a sale that was not forced. The value of the *Lyrna* at the termination of the salvage was assessed by Brandon J at £55,000. In *The Tullikki* ND 1975, p. 203 and 1979, p. 111 the proceeds obtained at the forced sale was accepted as basis for calculating ship's contributing value to general average whereas the court used the value insured in assessing the claim against hull underwriters.

the most accurate test, he thinks, based on actual sales of vessels similar to that of the salved vessel. Reproduction cost less depreciation is a method sometimes used.[16] Last in the list comes the insurance value which may be taken into consideration but does not have much weight as evidence.[17]

Rodière[18] points out that in assessing the value of the vessel salved decisions often take into account the insured value but "il faut préciser qu'il n'y là qu'une indication, même si la valeur avait été agrée par les assureurs". The market is what counts, Le Clerc[19] says, not the subjective value nor the amount for which the vessel is insured "encore que celle-ci soient intéressentes à connaitre à titre indicatif". Schimmering[20] also takes exception to the insured value: "Massgebend ist vielmehr der gemeine Handelswert am Ort und zur Zeit der beendeten Bergung oder Hilfesleitung". Berlingieri[21] says that it has often been sustained that the vessel's value is the insured one. This value can be followed only as an indication or presumption. It is a contractual agreement without consequence to a third party. The valuation may, moreover, be very different from the true market value if there are market fluctuations.

After this round trip let us return to Scandinavia.

In his work about salvage Braekhus[22] discusses ship's value for salvage purposes. He points out that for ordinary commercial vessels, not tied up by charterparties, it should be comparatively easy to assess ship's value. Brokers will be able to tell what the market value is. They will indicate the sound value. Deduction should be made for ship's damage. Tender for the repairs, vouchers for the actual cost of repairs will be used as evidence. Where there is no free market value because the authorities have fixed a ceiling price for vessels or a maximum freight the situation may become more complicated. A lengthy discussion ensued following the decision of the Norwegian Government in 1940 to impose a maximum price on ships, the price

16. *The Olaf Scheel* ND 1976, p. 389.

17. *The Sally* ND 1979, p. 163. Salvage of former cargo vessel converted into lighter. "While ship's value may not be as high as the insurance sum of Nowegian kroner 900,000 this amount probably gives a better idea of her true value than the proceeds of NKR 20,000", the court said.

The Feiebas ND 1980, p. 78. Price obtained at sale of vessel NKR 3,315,000 preferred to amount insured NKR 1,300,000 is assessing salved value.

18. Rodière and Lureau, p. 207.

19. Le Clerc, p. 226.

20. Schimmering, *ibid.*

21. Berlingieri, p. 193.

22. Braekhus, 747: 1 and 747: 2.

not to exceed the value prevailing on 8 April 1940, the day before the German occupation of Norway. Braekhus refers to that discussion.[23] Eventually he says the Norwegian Price Authorities decided in December 1950 that the ceiling price should not operate for salvage purposes. Salvage remunerations should be fixed without regard to the artificial price.

The agreed value of the hull policy cannot automatically be used, Braekhus says. That value may be well above the market value. If the ship salved is a specialized vessel it can be difficult to ascertain what her market value is. Is a prospective buyer to be found at all? The value may have to be arrived at by capitalizing her earnings[24] (the commercial value) or by taking the cost of replacement according to prevailing prices less depreciation for wear and tear (the technical value). For vessels that are not used for commercial purposes (warships, lightships, training vessels) only the technical method can be used. For specialized vessels used for commercial purposes there is, according to Braekhus, much to be said in favour of using the technical method where no market value can be found. This is because the commercial value of such vessels to a large extent depends on the contracts made by the owner. These elements should be left out of account.

Chartered vessels, and the Scandinavian view

In the section dealing with charterparties and ship's value (see Chapter 6) I indicated the attitudes of Braekhus and Beyer and also the decision of the Norwegian Supreme Court, *The Stigstad* case, to the effect that ship's value should be assessed free of commitments. I believe, however, that the matter is sufficiently important to warrant it being considered also in the context of salvage. Braekhus takes up the problems connected with vessels that are chartered, for a period of time or for consecutive voyages, and suggests that for some time ship's earnings are insulated from the fluctuation of the ordinary freight

23. ND 1942. 177–180 (Fride) 1944. 289–295 (Beyer) 1945. 21–23 (Magnus) 1946. 161–185. See also Thorbjørnsen in book cited.

24. I entertain some doubt as to whether the earnings of a vessel are that easily looked into. I would have thought that in most cases they remain a well guarded business secret. A general idea of earnings of vessels similar to the salved one should be comparatively easy to find, whereas the actual earnings of the salved vessel at the time which is the result of her owner's skill and luck will, if possible, be kept under lock and key. We know that in collision claims the "demurrage" items is the one which it takes the parties most time on which to agree.

market. At the time of the salvage operations the earnings under the charter may be above or below the going market rate. The ship in the hands of her owner may be worth more or less with her charter than without. Braekhus cites the case of *The Sunlong*.[25] At the time of the salvage, December 1954, the *Sunlong* was worth 3½ million Norwegian kroner without her charter, running until Nov/Dec 1956. This charter was a good one. The owners had bought her shortly before the accident for N. Kr. 5,100,000. What was the salved value in that case? Should one take into account the added value that the good charterparty gave to the ship? Is it possible to adopt a medium solution, only taking into account the added value a profitable charter gives to the ship, using her value free of commitments when the ship is contracted below the market rates? "English practice" points towards the medium solution, Braekhus says. In *The San Onofre* (1917) (17 Asp. MLC 74, referred to at some length above in the section on charterparties) the value free of charter, some £370,000 was taken as a basis; the vessel was chartered for 14 years ahead for a low freight and was with her charter only worth £160,000. In *The Castor* (1932) 43 Ll.L.Rep. 261, the values without and with charter were respectively £72,820 and £85,000. This latter value was found to be the decisive one. Braekhus then goes on to say that for Norwegian law the situation is not definitely decided. Practice, however, certainly points in the direction that it is ship's value free of charter that is relevant.[26] He is in favour of that attitude. As pointed out in the case of *The Sunlong* it is the salving of real or actual values (*realverdier*) that counts. The best expression of this is the market value free of charterparty. He takes the case of two vessels abandoned by their crew where the only salvage vessel in the region is capable of salving only one of the two. Vessel "A" is worth three million and vessel "B" two million. "A" is free of charter whereas "B" is chartered and worth four million with her charter. "The salvage rules ought to be framed in such a way that the salvor in this case is encouraged to salve vessel "A" rather than "B". The fact that the owner of the "B" loses the charterparty with the loss of his vessel is balanced by the charterer of the "B" obtaining an equivalent advantage."

Braekhus concludes his observation by pointing out that if favourable charterparties were to be allowed to increase the value of a vessel then a poor charterparty must be allowed to reduce such value.

---

25. ND 1954: 664.
26. The cases of *The Sunlong* (ND 1954, p. 664); *The Cranus* (ND 1956, p. 520); *The Kong Alf* (ND 1945, p. 499, esp. p. 460); *The Parkhaven* (ND 1920, p. 106).

A situation may well occur where such a reduction would make the vessel have no value to the owner. One would then have to introduce a rule to the effect that in such a case the charterer should pay the salvage remuneration in respect of the charterparty that is advantageous to him. This would break up the traditional framework of the salvage institution.

I have dwelt at some length on what Braekhus says because it indicates the prevalent views held in Scandinavia, especially in respect of the relation between ship's value and her charterparty. I also refer to what has been said already under the section devoted to charterparties and ship's value above (See Chapter 6).

Number of salvage cases dealt with in London

When starting out on this section I described some practical situations and experiences. One experience I did not specially point out—I had perhaps better do it here—is the fact that in Sweden the parties generally agree on the salvage remuneration to be paid without resorting to an outsider.[27] This is not the situation everywhere. Not all salvage cases are dealt with amicably. The salvage contract used mostly is *Lloyd's Form of Salvage Agreement*, the LOF. The LOF, both before and after the revised version of 1980, referred the parties to arbitration in London. From the 1980 LOF I quote Clause 1*b*: "The contractors' remuneration shall be fixed by arbitration in London in the manner herein prescribed and any difference arising out of this Agreement or the operation thereunder shall be referred to arbitration in the same way . . .".

Clause 1*d* says: "This Agreement shall be governed by and arbitration thereunder shall be in accordance with English law".

In the five-year period 1968 to 1972 a total of 602 cases were arbitrated in London under the LOF form and in the five-year period 1980 to 1984, 618 cases. This means some 120 cases per year or more than two per week. The number of appeals heard in the first period was 235 and in the second period 296, thus an average of 47 and 59 cases for the respective periods.

These figures show the great number of arbitrations in salvage

---

27. *Cf.* in this respect a letter in 1974 from a Swedish hull underwriter to a cargo underwriter abroad where it is said: "However, Swedish courts have practically no knowledge at all of salvage cases, the last one now being about ten years old, and therefore the advantage of a court trial in our opinion would have been very dubious".

cases where English law applies and where the arbitrators thus have to follow English law in respect of ship's value.[28]

It is thus not possible to dismiss the different method of ship's valuation as of little practical importance. On the contrary, owing to the arbitration clause English law will be made to apply in many cases where but for that clause it would not.

Evaluation of the English valuation method in salvage cases

In the section on collision recovery I have taken exception to assessing ship's value with commitments. I do not like it any better in connection with salvage.

I shall try to marshall my arguments and will present them as follows.

The value of the *property salved* is the *security* and limit of the salvage remuneration.[29] If salvors have to resort to a forced sale of the vessel to obtain satisfaction how could a supposed increased value owing to a favourable charterparty come their way? The charterparty would not survive such a sale. If the vessel is sold by a voluntary sale the survival of the charterparty will depend on negotiations between the seller, the buyer and the charterer. Assuming the court is aware of the outcome of such negotiations is the result to be taken into account in the sense that ship's value would be different depending on whether the three parties agree to make the charterparty survive or expire? I doubt it.

The *logical* consequences of looking to ship's value with commitments would have it that the court should take into consideration not only the long term charterparty that is profitable to the shipowner but also to those that happen to be unremunerative

28. The President of the Gothenburg Court of Appeal, G Lagergren, said in "Erfarenheter som Internationell Skiljedomare" a paper read before the seminar of the Stockholm Chamber of Commerce in May 1973: "The English in this field have an additional worry in that the arbitrator in the course of an arbitration may either on his own initiative or at the request of one of the parties' 'state a special case', the term used to the court on a question of law. He can be forced to do so in certain circumstances by a party who wishes it done. In this way a party may delay an arbitration considerably. All this has the effect that in international contracts the parties avoid having arbitrations in London" (my translation). The figures indicated hardly support this view in respect of salvage cases.

29. *Cf.* Wildeboer, p. 204: ". . . the value of the goods salvaged constitutes the fund which serves for remuneration and indemnification of the salvors . . . This means, *inter alia*, that the value in damaged condition is concern; moreover it means that the objective value is concerned not the subjective value which the ship and the cargo represents for the owners".

and make the latter reduce ship's value to something less than her value as a free ship. This is not so, at any rate there is no certainty that the English court would do so.

The *legal* objection as I see it is that the ship and the charterparty do not form one unit. They are not closely linked together like Siamese twins. As is explained under the section on ship's value for credit purposes efforts to make the charterparty automatically follow the ship when sold have been unsuccessful, nationally and internationally.

I submit that to make the commitments of the vessel under her charterparty an element in assessing her value is to introduce a purely *arbitrary element*, into the calculation.

Why only look at the charterparty? The charterparty is the result of the skill (and sometimes luck) of the shipowner in influencing the value of his ship. Why not look at other elements as well? The price of bunker oil has gone up steeply.[30] Why are bunkering contracts of some duration not contracted at a low (or high) price made to have a bearing on ship's value to her owner? If so, should not the long term charterparty be set off against the long term bunkering contract? If the charterparty is a profitable one to the shipowner and the bunkering contract not, or vice versa, should the balance affect ship's value? And what of the financing of the ship; are the terms costly or not? Should that be taken into account?

The *encouragement of salvors* should not be based on a concept that what they have saved is worth more than they can obtain if the salved ship was sold. And one should not lose sight of the fact that the salved values come at the end of the list of elements to be considered when assessing the salvage remuneration. Moreover, the salvage industry manages to survive even where the English method of assessing ship's value is not followed.

The *International uniformity* was the goal of the 1910 Convention on salvage. A special national rule in that connection, albeit an English one, will not help towards this goal. It should be borne in mind that it proved possible to introduce in the York/Antwerp Rules 1974 on

---

30. In his paper "Currency, mortgages and charters" read at the Seatrade Money and Ships' Conference in 1974 B Rappaport drew attention to other elements than the charter to be taken into account: "For it should be plain to all of us—those who order ships built in foreign shipyards, who purchase our ships and mortgage them; who charter and operate ships, repair and maintain them or do anything else with them in the world markets and in the world's ports—that the news is out loud and clear: *spiralled inflationary costs with bunker not banker the chief evil* (my italics) . . .". *Cf.* however change of trend in oil prices signalled on p. 26, fn. 7.

general average a rule that positively excluded charterparty, good or poor, from any influence on ship's value for general average purposes. Speaking in 1973, thus before the amendment of the York/Antwerp Rules on this point in 1974 the Chairman of the Association of Average Adjusters N G Hudson said:[31]

If one adds to this the fact [that the salvors enjoy preferential lien on the property salved] "that the law of salvage, dealing with the quantification of the salvor's award (based upon the value obtaining at the time and place where the salvor's services end and the salvor's lien is maintainable) has historically speaking been the prerequisite of the law of admiralty, while matters of general average have been dealt with in the Commercial Courts, it is perhaps not surprising that legal practitioners have tended to emphasize the points of difference rather than the points of similarity.

What has been said, seen in the light that the rules on general average have since been amended in the sense that the charterparty should not be taken into account, indicates that general average should not constitute an insurmountable obstacle for a change. On the contrary, the change with respect to general average should make it much easier for the courts to change their attitude now that they will be aware, as will be explained under the section on general average, that even if for salvage purposes ship's value with commitments is set at 20,000 the salvage remuneration allowed in general average will be apportioned over value of cargo and ship's value free of commitments which may be 15,000 instead of the 20,000.

There is a further difficulty that has to be overcome to obtain international uniformity on this point. Would it be necessary to change the law of England to reach that goal? My understanding is that the House of Lords can "exercise its undoubted power not to adhere to a previous decision of its own".[32,33] I am not even sure the

31. Association of Average Adjuster Report of General Meeting held on 10 May 1973.

32. *Cf.* in this respect the decision of the Judicial Committee on the Privy Council in *Geelong Harbour Trust Commissioners* v. *Gibbs Bright & Co (The Octavian)* [1974] 1 Lloyd's Rep 344) where Lord Diplock said: "... there is, however, a wider consideration which would make their Lordships reluctant to interfere with the decision of the High Court (of Australia) on a matter of this kind. If the legal process is to retain the confidence of the nation the extent to which the High Court exercises its undoubted power not to adhere to a previous decision of its own must be consonant with the consensus of opinion of the public, of the elected legislature and of the judiciary as to the proper balance between the respective roles of the legislature and of the judiciary as lawmakers. Even among those nations where legal system derives from the common law of England this consensus may vary from country to country and from time to time. It may be influenced by the Federal or unitary nature of the constitution and whether it is written or unwritten, by the legislative procedure in Parliament, by

House of Lords would have to go that far in view of the fact that *The Edison* case (quoted in the section on charterparties) as I read it, gives sufficient liberty of action to the House of Lords to allow for a change of direction if and when it is convinced by these and other arguments, presented with the usual skill and brilliance of a QC.

Application of method of valuation

In the section on collision recovery I dealt with the problem of what is the proper claim for a vessel that has become a total loss. In salvage cases the vessel is still there, in most cases in a damaged condition. It is not enough to state that ship's value had better be assessed free of commitments; this still does not say what that value is, nor what method should be used to arrive at that value. The pragmatic section above (*vide supra* Salvage p. 87 *et seq.*) contains some solutions resorted to in practice. Like Norris/Benedict (*vide supra* Salvage p. 92 *et seq.*) I believe that out of his seven "models" the market value less cost of repairs is the most accurate test. If the vessel is too specialized to fit in into the general tonnage market or if there is no such market at the time or at the place where salvage operation came to an end other solutions must be found. As the next best solution the replacement cost less yearly depreciation might perhaps be made to work. The difficulties in applying the replacement or reproduction method when it comes to ships I have indicated already in the section on collision recovery (*vide supra* Collision p. 97). They will serve to explain my lukewarm recommendation of it in salvage cases.

---

the case with which parliamentary time can be found to effect amendments in the law which concern only a small minority of citizens, by the extent to which Parliament has been in the habit of intervening to reverse judicial decisions by legislation; but most of all by the underlying political philosophy of the particular nation as to the appropriate limits of law making of a non-elected judiciary . . .".

33. *Cf.* also Philip H James, p. 11.

I I

General Average

General average is all over the world based on the York/Antwerp Rules. The 1950 version of the York/Antwerp Rules were amended in some respects at the Hamburg Conference of the CMI in April 1974. A significant change was introduced in the new rules which is of particular interest for the purpose of this study.

Introduction

Rule XVII of the York/Antwerp Rules 1974 says in respect of ship's value at the termination of the adventure:

"The value of the ship shall be assessed without taking into account the beneficial or detrimental effect of any demise or time charterparty to which the ship may be committed."

Thus the problem of valuation "with commitments", "free of commitments" and the like is happily disposed of so far as general average goes. The other elements that make up ship's value for general average purposes will have to be looked into as carefully under the new as under the earlier versions of the York/Antwerp Rules.

Writing in 1923 about ascertaining the ship's value for general average purposes Congdon[1] pointed out that this was difficult "owing to the ever varying conditions of their age, build and type, and the systems employed by surveyors and others in arriving at their values differ".

He then goes on to explain different methods; the original cost or, if unknown, the estimated costs less a percentage for annual depreciation. This he rejects as estimated annual depreciation might in some cases reduce ship's value to practically nothing. Vessels of the same age, build and type may differ in value depending on their upkeep. Others use the sale prices of similar vessels "making such alterations in respect of the value sought as the difference, if any, in

---

1. E W Congdon: *General Average*, 2nd edn., New York 1923, p. 168.

the comparison may warrant". Congdon prefers some other methods to those indicated and suggests ascertaining the cost of building one of the same type less a reasonable amount for wear and tear dependent on her age and upkeep. "There is", he says, "however, no general rule which will meet all cases, and even more difficulty is encountered in determining the values here of foreign nationalities than those owned and registered in the United States.[2]

The development towards the use of the market value where English law does not apply is explained by Buglass writing before the York/Antwerp Rules 1974 were adopted. He says:[3]

"In the United States it is customary to base the vessel's contributory value on the sale prices of similar vessels which have been sold by their owners within a recent period, making such adjustments as may be necessary reflect the age and condition of the particular vessel being valued; "the worth of the thing is the price it will bring." (*The Blanche C Pendleton*, 1924 AMC, 382 (4 CCA ED Va).[4/5] It has never been the practice to take into consideration any charterparty under which the vessel may be operating—whether it be remunerative or otherwise. In other words, the value generally used is the value of the vessel in the open market as if she were a free vessel without reference to the benefit which might accrue under her existing contractual obligations. This is in accord with the law of damages, it being fundamental that the measure of damages to be applied is the market value of the lost ship if it has a market value at the time of destruction. This value is to be established by contemporaneous sales. Other evidence of value, such as reproduction cost depreciated, may be resorted to only where no market value can be established (*Standard Oil Co* v. *Southern Pacific Co* 268 US 146). As already indicated, any repairs effected at port of refuge are deducted.

As for ship's value the situation in the UK seems clear enough under the York/Antwerp Rules 1950. The Advisory Committee, of the Association of Average Adjusters said that it was "of the opinion that the test that is laid down in the case of *The Hohenzollern* [(1906) 10 Asp. MLC 236, at p. 339], namely that the value is what the ship is worth in her damaged state to her owners. If a vessel is under a time charter and the time charter attaches to that ship the value of the charter is an element in the ship."

In view of the change introduced in Rule XVII of the York/Antwerp Rules 1974 I take leave of the problem of the charterparty and ship's value and address myself to the three other elements that are to be taken into account for general average purposes: (i) the place where the voyage ends; (ii) the net value; and (iii) the time element, "the termination of the adventure".

---

2. Ibid., p. 169.
3. L J Buglass, 2nd edn. p. 182, (3rd edn., p. 272).
4/5. The words also appear in the English case *The Clyde* (1856) as already indicated.

Place where the voyage ends

In most cases the ship's valuer will not ask for the place where the ship is lying, still less indicate it in his valuation certificate. It would thus appear safe to say that the market value of a vessel is the same whether the voyage terminates in port A or B, in Rotterdam or Casablanca. Geography has no bearing on ship's value! Is that so? Never and in no circumstances? The assertion is much too wide.

(i) *Effect of disrupted market*

As said elsewhere Norway during the Second World War introduced maximum prices for ships whereas France at the end of that war refused licences for the purchase of vessels from abroad which pushed up the values of French ships in the home market. What effect should such measures be allowed to have on ships' values for general average purposes? Would it be correct to say the ship's value should be different depending on whether the voyage where the ship met with a general average was outgoing from France or Norway or homebound; that is to say outbound toward a free market or homebound towards a regulated one?[6] During the First World War the Netherlands introduced maximum freights. Should Dutch vessels then have been valued differently from other ships?

Not only official decree can upset the international price structure. The market may be different in two countries, even neighbouring ones at that, for other reasons. The following will illustrate the point.

At the meeting of the Nordic Average Adjusters in Helsingfors in 1954 the matter of international disparity in prices was raised. I translate from the Swedish minutes.[7]

"Mr Hasselrot (Stockholm) explained that owing to special circumstances in Finland such as inflation, scarcity of tonnage, etc., ship's values are higher than elsewhere. Thus in 1951 it happened that a Swedish liner service vessel was taxed at destination Helsingfors at Sw. Kr. 2,700,000 whereas in Stockholm her value was estimated as Sw. Kr. 2,100,000. (Hull Policy value Sw. Kr. 2,300,000). According to the York/Antwerp Rules the value in the country where the voyage ends should be used for calculation of the contributing values. What this actually means is not always easy to say. The easy way out—to use the average of the two values—was not adopted. But was it really true to say that ship's value on arrival at Stockholm Monday,

6. See chapter on Collision.
7. Protocol from Nordiska Dispashörsmötet 1954 (not in print).

Wednesday and Friday should be taken as Sw. Kr. 2,100,000 and in Helsingfors Tuesday, Thursday and Saturday Sw. Kr. 2,700,000? In this case the value used in the statement was taken as Sw. Kr. 2,300,000 [figure of the valued hull policy] that is to say the amount that was a risk to the shipowner this being understood to express the worldmarket price.

In the ensuing discussion it was said:

Mr Skovgaard-Petersen (Copenhagen): The adjusters must be at liberty to decide; according to Rule XVII it is over the true net values at the end of the voyage that general average shall be apportioned.

Mr Hasselrot: Yes, but according to Rule G it is the value of the ship at the place where the voyage ends that counts.

Mr Strøm-Olsen (Oslo): In Norway regulations about maximum prices were introduced after the occupation 9 April 1940. The Norwegian Supreme Court has decided, however, that in assessing ship's value the price regulating provisions should be disregarded. [This assertion should, I take it, be understood to refer to general average and salvage, *cf.* above p. 94].

This was an argument in favour of using world market prices.

Mr Middelfart (Trondheim): If the vessel can be sold at a higher price at destination (than at port of departure) that value appears to be the correct one.

Mr Hasselrot: The price the vessel can fetch in Helsingfors, cannot be the only decisive factor. One must take into account the costs of replacement. The fact that such a ship cannot be bought in Finland speaks in favour of adopting world market prices and also ships' values in most countries base their estimate on the prices in the international market.

Mr Tybjerg (Copenhagen) declared that as long as there was no judgement at hand that clarified the issue one should agree on using the world market price as the proper value."

Another example of the influence of geography was pointed out by S Andersen in 1924.[8] He said it was well known that the majority of German charterparties and bills of lading "today" (i.e. the early 1920s) contained provisions that accorded the shipowners the right to have ship's value assessed and the general average statement drawn up in Germany. The reasons for it were simple enough, he said. Shipowners obtained a value for the ship which was extraordinarily low and the majority of the general average expenditure accordingly lay on the shoulders of cargo. Then we have *The Remøy*, albeit a salvage case (see above, p. 89) where the court had to form an opinion on ship's value in damaged condition, the vessel lying far off the beaten track.

The Non-Separation Agreement form used most says in respect of

---

8. S Andersen, Svendborg: *Om Forsikring af fragt, Nordisk Försäkrings Tidskrift* 1924 and also Hasselrot, p. 188.

values: "The basis of contribution to general average involved shall be the values on delivery at the original destination but where none of her cargo is carried forward in the vessel she shall contribute on the basis of her actual value on the date she completes discharge of her cargo".

This means that under this clause the ship will in some cases contribute to general average on the basis of her value in a port of refuge, perhaps far off the beaten track as in *The Remøy* case.

While I believe it is still true to say that the basic value from which to start the calculation of ship's value for general average purposes will be identical whether the voyage comes to an end in say Rotterdam or Gothenburg, the above examples tell us that geography may sometimes influence the value of the ship for general average purposes and for other purposes as well.

Leaving aside the different methods of assessing ship's sound value discussed in the market value section and elsewhere, attention is draw to the words "actual net values" in Rule XVII.

(ii) *Value at destination as illustrated by old Swedish cases*

According to the Swedish Maritime Code in its version up to 1967 and the master in general average cases had to ask for a survey of his ship where ship and cargo parted company. The surveyor had to estimate the cost of repairs and indicate ship's value in damaged condition (Arts. 40 and 207). This way of arriving at the actual net value was none too easy as will appear from the following, albeit rather, old, cases.

After grounding the English vessel *Manningham* called at Stockholm as port of refuge. Surveyors estimated the cost of repairs as Kr. 62,810 and her value in damaged condition as £3,200 = Kr. 58,200. At a voluntary sale the vessel fetched Kr. 36,100 and this amount the adjuster used as her contributing value in the general average statement, a decision that was upheld by the Stockholm City Court. The Supreme Court reached a different conclusion. The true value of the vessel, the sale of which by auction was not necessary, must be regarded as the value indicated at the survey arranged according to the provisions of law on 20 and 22 June 1897 or £3,200 equivalent to Kr. 58,200. For that reason the Supreme Court sent the case back to the adjuster for readjustment.[9]

I read this to mean that the court preferred the result of the experts'

9. NJA 1897, p. 596 *et seq.*

valuation to the proceeds obtained at the auction because it was a voluntary not a forced sale!

On her voyage from the Mediterranean to Scandinavian ports the *Norge* grounded and was taken to Lisbon. Cargo went forward to destination with another vessel. The ship was inspected and a value in damaged condition of Milreis 9,860 = Kr. 28,396.80 was indicated. Cargo interests asked for another survey. This report gave her a value in damaged condition as Milreis 26,460 = Kr. 76,240.80.

In the general average statement by the average adjuster of Stockholm the lower value of the two was used. The value arrived at the first survey was obviously a low one, especially when the insured value of 170,000 was taken into account. Every valuation was however subjective and thus open to different opinions. The cargo underwriters had not proved that the survey arranged at the request of the master by lawfully appointed surveyors was not correct and for that reason the adjuster did not accept the request of cargo underwriters. The City Court upheld the decision. On the matter being brought before the Supreme Court the Nedre Justitierevisionen said ". . . that the value of the vessel used by the adjuster in the statement was obviously too low since the vessel's true value in damaged condition before repairs was at least the amount fixed by the surveyors or Milreis 26,460 at 27.88 equivalent to Kr. 76,240.80 . . .". For that reason it was recommended that the said value should be accepted, which the Supreme Court did.[10]

This means the court, like the adjuster, used its discretionary power but reached a different conclusion.

The *Aberfoyle* grounded near Öland and was taken to Kalmar where her cargo was discharged and sold. The surveyor valued the vessel in damaged condition at some £6,000. The master protested against this figure. He took the vessel under her own power to Copenhagen where she was drydocked. A tender for repair amounting to £5,016 was accepted. Ship's value in damaged condition was estimated at £2,300. (Her insured value was £10,000). The average adjuster of Stockholm said that as the costs of repairs amounted to £5,200 the value indicated in Copenhagen was obviously too low. The value with which the ship should contribute to general average was the one given in Kalmar or £6,000. The City Court, however, accepted the Copenhagen value. The surveyors in Kalmar had made only a rough estimate of the costs of repairs.

The Supreme Court (a majority) found that "such circumstances were not at hand in the case to show that ship's value in damaged condition should be fixed differently from what is done in the adjustment according to the estimate made in Kalmar or £6,000" and upheld the adjustment.

Two judges (Cassel and Lilienberg) were of different opinion. "As said by the City Court at the survey and valuation made in Kalmar the surveyors had failed to estimate the damage caused by the grounding, which they should have done and calculate the cost of repair; in the circumstances ship's value in damaged condition cannot be said to be assessed in a reliable way by the said

10. NJA 1900, p. 2 *et seq.*

survey. As the survey and valuation made by duly appointed surveyors (in Copenhagen) is not shown to be incorrect in respect of ship's value in damaged condition I find no reason not to uphold the decision of the City Court".[11]

It is difficult to interpret this decision one way or the other because we do not know the sound value of the vessel that served as a basis for the estimates made or what other elements were made to bear on the different results arrived at.

The *Turret Age*, a British vessel, grounded and called at Stockholm as port of refuge where the voyage came to an end. the *Turret Age* was valued at £3,500 = Kr. 63,560 and was sold for £4,900. The average adjuster used the lower figure Kr. 63,560. the City Court and the Supreme Court upheld the decision.[12]

After a grounding the *Mannhem* called at Visby as port of refuge. Surveyors, who were duly appointed, estimated her value in damaged condition at Kr. 50,000, provided the diver's report on bottom damage on the whole proved correct. The *Mannhem* was taken to Norrköping and drydocked. Surveyors there said she was worth Kr. 37,000. The average adjuster used that value. The surveyors at Visby although dully appointed had not, he said, been in the position to know for certain the number of bottom plates that had to be renewed, nor the cost of repairs.

Cargo interests appealed. The survey at Norrköping they said had not been made pursuant to Art. 207 of the Maritime Code, the surveyors were not properly appointed, their task being merely to arrange the settlement between the shipowners and his hull underwriter. For these reasons and because the surveyors at Visby who took part in the surveys at Norrköping maintained their estimate cargo submitted the higher value of the two should be used. The City Court, however, upheld the decision of the average adjuster and the Nedre Justitierevisionen advised the Supreme Court to do likewise. This advice the Supreme Court did not follow. It did not accept as valid the reasons invoked by the average adjuster why the result of the Visby survey, made according to the provisions of Art. 207 of the Maritime Code, should be disregarded. Taking into account among other things the value for which the vessel was insured at the time of the grounding and the cost expended after the accident to put her in good and seaworthy condition the value of the ship in damaged condition as assessed in Visby was not too high. Ship's contributing value was to be taken as kr. 50,000.[13]

On reading these cases, especially *The Mannhem*, one is struck by two things. First, the nearly impossible task imposed on the surveyors. They were asked at an early stage, sometimes even before the vessel

11. NJA 1902, p. 102, *et seq.* ND 1902, p. 121 *et seq.*
12. NJA 1904, p. 322.
13. Dispache 9 April 1897, Stockholm Rådhusrätt 3 March 1898 HD 17 October 1898. The case does not appear in the printed reports. It is reproduced here from archives held by Riksarkivet.

had been in dock, to estimate the cost of repair and assess ship's value in damaged condition. And secondly that in spite of these difficulties and the errors that might ensue, the courts were prepared to attach great importance to the fact that the surveyors were duly appointed according to the provisions in law. This formal approach to evidence submitted sounds rather old fashioned. The courts of today would feel free to weigh the evidence submitted on its intrinsic value only. The Swedish average adjuster always has.[14]

What is now the normal procedure to arrive at the net value? The sound value as given by experts, less value of estimated or actual cost of repair is the method probably resorted to in most cases. Obviously the sound value will have to be reduced with damage sustained at the last voyage but also with an unrepaired damage due to previous accidents that existed at the termination of the voyage. In some places the experts are invited to indicate ship's value in damaged conditions.[15] The courts will not necessarily accept the price obtained at a voluntary sale of the vessel[16] nor will they automatically follow the price obtained at a forced sale.[17]

(iii)   *Vessel removed from one place to another or immobilized*

What about the cost of removing the vessel under tow from the port where the voyage came to an end to a port of repair whence she is unable to proceed under her own power? Does it form part of the cost of repair? Should it be added to the repair bill if shown separately and the total deducted from the sound value? Will the answer depend on whether the tender for repairs includes them or not? The solution cannot be made to depend on some such technicalities. If the vessel has to be removed because there are no repair facilities where the voyage terminates it seems natural to put the charges of removal on a par with the cost of repairs, whether included in the tender or not, and make deduction for it. If repairs can be made where the voyage came to an end the vessel will not be removed to another port unless the tender for repairs, together with the cost of removal, are less than the local tender submitted; thus the problem of removal cost will not arise.

14. *Cf.* Hasselrot, p. 187.

15. AIDE Cambridge, p. 26 ". . . it has always been a fixed rule in my country (the Netherlands) or let me say, in the port of Rotterdam, to depart from the value in damaged condition".

16. *Cf. The Manningham* quoted above, p. 105.

17. *Cf. The Lyrna* [1978] 2 Lloyd's Rep 27 and *The Tullikki* ND 1979. p. 111.

What about the situation where the voyage comes to an end at a place, be it the original port of desination or at a port of refuge, because the vessel is damaged to such an extent that she cannot be removed to a port of repair and cannot be repaired on the spot either permanently or temporarily? Is it then possible to establish the net value of the vessel for general average purposes by assessing her sound market value and deducting estimated cost of repairs? Will not the starting point be too much of a fiction? In theory the sound value less repair cost should give a correct result. But will it always? It will depend on the circumstances in each case. I have discussed some aspects of this situation in the section on salvage. I would say that the adjuster in that situation would very much like to have a cross check by asking the owner or his hull underwriter to invite tenders for the vessel "as is". Tenders may not give rise to competition between prospective buyers. It may well prove to be anything but a seller's market. The price actually obtained will usually be the one to follow for general average purposes as the ship in the circumstances described represents only a scrap value.[18]

At the termination of the adventure

Having dealt with the place where the voyage ends, the net value we now come to the third element to take account when assessing ship's value for general average purposes, the time factor "at the termination of the adventure". For the purpose of ascertaining the value of a ship the time factor is nothing new or revolutionary. A value to be used for assessing salvage remuneration or for a collision recovery has to take into account the value at a specific time. Not necessarily at a certain date in the month but the value as it is

---

18. In my experience a combination of skillful bargaining followed by risky feats of seamanship to bring such a vessel to a port of repair has sometimes resulted in the reappearance of the vessel "fighting fit" at a later stage, much to the surprise of her former owners and hull underwriters. Those few cases are exceptions and do not affect what is said above about the sale price as the decisive factor.

Cf. in this connection Hasselrot, p. 189 *et seq.* For a vessel that is condemned the value at public auction should be accepted even where experts indicate another value in their certificate. The result obtained at a private sale is also acceptable if one is satisfied that the sale is a genuine one and not of a fictitious character. When the vessel is not condemned and the sale thus not warranted by events Swedish courts will not feel bound to accept the result of the sale if reliable experts indicate another value.

The value insured can only serve as a guide towards the true value; in case of dual valuation the total loss value, i.e. the lower of the two values indicated in the policy, may prove nearer ship's true value than the other.

supposed to exist during a certain limited period of time. This is indicated in valuation instruments by "during the latter part of the month of . . ." or some similar expression. The exact date, "the termination of the adventure" may sometimes have to be taken more literally than that. Outside events may bring about a sudden and steep rise in ship's value. The closing of the Suez Canal is one example. It had a bearing on the tanker tonnage generally and on the particular tanker in hand; so had the reopening of it. Likewise outbreak of hostilities somewhere on the globe or the cessation of them may affect the value of the ship. Did the termination of the adventure occur before or after that date? The valuation will in such cases have to take into account the time factor within a more exact and precise term than is otherwise necessary.

Concluding observations

The report of the Working Group on Ship's Value appointed by the AIDE ended its report by saying: ". . . generally speaking the assessing of ship's value for general average purposes had not caused major problems for the adjuster. The amendment introduced in the York/Antwerp Rules 1974 . . . has served to eliminate one difficulty and promote uniformity of practice."[19]

19. Working Report of 14 March 1978 to the AIDE Conference Cambridge, p. 72. *Cf.* however, the plenary session where attention was brought to a case where "some seven opinions were obtained from reputable expert valuers both in the UK and on the Continent of Europe, all of which quoted different figures. Of these the highest was more than 140 in excess of the lowest". AIDE Cambridge, p. 22.

12

Limitation of Liability[1]

All maritime nations grant permission to the owner of a seagoing ship to limit his liability in respect of certain claims, among them claims for collision damages.

Uniformity of the rules[2]

The initiative to arrive at uniform rules of limitation was taken by the CMI in 1899. These efforts have continued. The world has seen three Conventions on limited liability, one of 1924, the next of 1957 and the last one of 1976. Having on 1 December 1985 obtained the necessary 12 ratifications the 1976 Convention enters into force on 1 December 1986.[3] Both the 1957 and 1976 Conventions calculate the limitation according to a certain figure of ship's tonnage, the "tonnage rule". States that have not ratified or acceded to any of these conventions use ship's value in one form or another as the basis for calculation of the limitation amount; among such states at the time of writing (1985) are the USA and the People's Republic of China.[4]

Comparison of the USA and the 1976 Convention limitation system

The survey referred to in fn. 4 illustrates the working of the two systems in respect of the vessel *Eve*, a dry cargo vessel of 35,000 tons.

---

1. This chapter is entirely rewritten.

2. Limited liability in respect of cargo loss or damage, passenger claims, oil pollution damage and nuclear damage are outside the scope of this study.

3. The 12 are the following: Bahamas, Benin, Denmark, Finland, France, Japan, Liberia, Norway, Spain, Sweden, United Kingdom and Yemen.

4. From the survey *Limited Liability in Collision Cases* by K Pineus and H G Röhreke, (Lloyd's of London Press Ltd, 1984) it appears that besides China and the USA the legislation in the following states take into account in one way or another ship's value for limitation purposes: Argentina, Brazil, Colombia, Greece, Italy, Mexico, Peru, Philippines and the USSR.

Her limited liability in respect of claims for loss of property would be her value at the end of the voyage.

<table>
<tr><td>taken as</td><td align="right">$9,000,000[5]</td></tr>
<tr><td>and her voyage freight</td><td align="right">300,000[6]</td></tr>
<tr><td></td><td align="right">$9,300,000</td></tr>
</table>

Assuming the *Eve* had suffered no damage owing to the collision or such other events that made her owner petition for limitation of liability, the amount of $9,300,000 is her limited liability in respect of damage to property under the law of the USA. Claimants for loss of life or personal injury have a guarantee for their claims based on $420 per ton. Thus for the owners of the *Eve* a maximum liability of $14,700,000 was specially set aside for this type of claim and independent of whether the *Eve* was lost or severely damaged.

Under the 1976 Convention the limited liability, based on a somewhat sophisticated tonnage rule, is expressed in SDR; for the benefit of those States that still have to use the Poincaré franc the equivalent in this unit is indicated. The limited liability of *Eve* in respect of damages for property would be SDR 5,718,500 (or $5,835,200)[6a] and in Poincaré francs it would be 85,500,000 or $5,816,350. In respect of claims for loss of life or personal injury the limited liability of the *Eve* would be SDR 11,824,000 (or $12,065,325) or if the Poincaré franc has to be used 177,500,000 Poincaré francs equivalent to $12,040,850.[6b]

---

5. *Cf. Ernest Pettus* v. *Jones and Lauglin Steel Corp.* 1972 AMC, 170 US DC Penn, where it is said *inter alia*, "A shipowner may limit his liability to the value of his interest in the vessel although he carries liability insurance in excess of such value".

6. The concept of freight, even time-charter freight, as an altogether separate entity not incorporated in ship's value is indicated by Jacobs commenting on the 1879 Belgian Maritime Law dealing with *inter alia* limitation based on the *fortune de mer* coupled with the *abandonment* system. ". . . si le navire est loué à l'année ou pour une série d'anées, le propriétaire fera l'abandon d'une de ce loyer global, proportionnée à la durée du voyage pendant lequel est née l'obligation dont il se dégage par l'abandon". Jacob No. 72.

6a. The conversion into US dollars of the SDR and the Poincaré franc as shown in the text is based on the rate of exchange at the time when this was written (September 1985).

6b. On the value of the Poincaré franc see articles in *Journal of Maritime Law and Commerce* by A J Mendelsohn (Oct 1973), T C M Asser (July 1974) and P P Heller (Oct 1974) also articles by S Royer (*Nederlands Juristenblad*, 73/20 May 1973) and by P Y Nicolas (*Droit Maritime Français*, 1980, p. 579).

"... the interest of such owner in such vessel"

The words quoted above reproduce the wording of the American statute.[7] They look clear and unambiguous. Are they? Perhaps not quite.

(i) When the vessel is sold does the interest of such owner comprise the proceeds obtained in respect of ship's bunkers when these are supplied by charterers? The charterers have successfully vindicated their right to such proportion of the total proceeds before English courts.[8] I should be surprised if the outcome would be different anywhere else.

(ii) Sometimes more vessels than one are put together and the total of their value made to constitute the limitation amount. This follows from the application of the flotilla rule concept. I have given much thought to whether a full explanation of that rule has its proper place in this study on ship's value. I have reached the conclusion that it has not. If only vessel A is liable with its value or whether also the value of vessel B should be taken into account belongs to a study of the law of limitation, not of ship's value. As a gesture towards those who may have liked to find a full exposé of the flotilla rule appear in this study I suggest some legal writings on the subject and some cases that deal with the problem.[9]

Evaluation of the two systems

Under the 1976 Convention rules the limited liability of the *Eve* would remain the same whether she is lost or severely damaged at the event that made her owner invoke limited liability. Under the law of the USA the limited liability of the *Eve* would be reduced by her loss or damage sustained; only the loss of life or personal injury claims are made independent of ship's value.

---

7. Liability of owner. Originally enacted in 1851, amended in 1873, 1935 and 1936. Act for Limitation of vessel owner's liability (46 USCA §§ 181–189).

8. *The Saint Anna* [1980] 1 Lloyd's Rep 180. *The Span Terza* [1984] 1 Lloyd's Rep 119. *Cf.* however *The Silia* [1981] 2 Lloyd's Rep 534.

9. S Braekhus in ND 1949, p. 633, which also has a very full bibliography and list of cases; Smeesters and Winkelmolen, No. 130; Jacob, p. 518 *et seq.*

See also the following American case: *Cross Contracting Co* v. Law 197 (AMC US Ct of App, p. 1008) and *Complaint of American Commercial Lines Inc. as Owner of the m.v. James L Hamilton and the Commercial Transport Corporation, as Owner of the m.v. La Salle and Inland Tugs as demise charterer and Bailee in possession of the said vessels for exoneration from or limitation of liability*, 1973 AMC, p. 319, USC, ED Kentucky and cases referred to in the decision.

From the practical point of view the 1976 Convention has some definite advantages over a limitation system based on ship's value. You know beforehand the maximum liability of the owner (and underwriter) in respect of third party risks. You avoid the difficulties we have come across in this study about how properly to assess ship's value, particularly her value in damaged condition. "Certainty instead of uncertainty" is a catchword sometimes used by underwriters selling their product. With the 1976 Convention you have the certainty; with the ship's value system the fall and rise in ships' values will affect the amount of the limited liability. It is for the legislator to decide whether this element of speculation should still form part of the limitation system.[10]

10. The "American method" may be encountered less frequently in practice as American courts have recently been reluctant to accept cases which have no connection with the USA. *Cf.*, e.g. *Piper Aircraft Co* v. *Gaynold Reyno* 1982 AMC (Sup Ct 1981) p. 214; also *Gahr Development Inc. of Panama* v. *Nedlloyd Marseilles* 1983 AMC 573 (USDC, ED La).

13

Summary and Conclusions

Summary

In the introduction it is pointed out that this study of ship's value is based mainly on Scandinavian and Anglo-American law with excursions into other legal systems.

The next section examines the various *models* and *methods* used to convey the meaning of "value". I try to show, without at this stage applying it to ships only, the meaning of terms like *market value, dividence value* (what the French call *Valeur de rendement*), *expectation value, replacement value, utility value* and the *liquidation or "slaughter value"*.

The section on the time element begins with some examples showing how rapid and important fluctuations in tonnage values do occur; this is in order to emphasize the importance of knowing the relevant time for assessing ship's value for particular purposes like hull insurance, credit, collision recovery, salvage, general average and limitation of liability.

Then follows a short section devoted to the technical approach in assessing ship's value.

I then address myself to the *market value* and how it applies to ships. The various elements of the ship that count are examined. The construction cost and its relation to market values are illustrated. What other elements the expert, i.e. the shipbroker, will have to take into account in arriving at the proper value is discussed and also illustrated by a set of questions that may be put to him in order to explain his assessment of ship's value.

The charterparty and its influence on ship's value are taken up in Chapter 6. Numerous vessels travel under charterparties. It is important to know whether the charterparty should be taken into account or not. Only in England is ship's value assessed "with commitments". The evaluation of the English method is left open to be examined in other sections.

Ship's value for credit purposes forms the subject of Chapter 7. While the objective value is used in practice two Swedish authors advocate that a high rate charterparty should be taken into account when assessing ship's value as a collateral for a credit granted rather than her value "free of commitments". In this connection the discussions held at the CMI conference in Athens in 1962 about registration of charterparties and their negative outcome are set out and also the fact that the survival of the charterparty in case of ship's sale was again discussed, but not adopted, at the revision of the Nordic Maritime Codes. I explain why I do not agree with the views about evaluation of ship "with commitments" as her value for credit purposes.

In Chapter 8 on hull insurance the value to be insured is discussed. What should be the "agreed value" in this connection? Discussions between hull underwriters are reported and also the interests of ship's creditors in having ship's full value adequately insured. The influence of the premiums and of the insurance conditions, among them the dual valuation and the hull interest provisions are examined. The unvalued policy and the assessment of the proper claim in case of loss under that type of policy conclude this section.

If the ship is lost owing to a collision and a claim against the counterparty is warranted what is the proper amount to claim for the ship lost? This problem was discussed at the CMI Conference in 1962. The different views put forward are looked into, the English concept of ship's value "with commitments" on the one hand, as against the principle of her value "free of commitments" on the other. According to those who held this latter view the profit claim was a valid one but constituted a separate item to be distinguished from ship's value. No final decision was reached. I take the opportunity to explain why I hold the "free of commitment" value to be the correct one and go on to show the practical difficulties in distributing the recovery obtained if the ship's value and her commitments are, so to say, baked into one loaf of bread. I wish to point out that the value of the ship forms part of the study of collision damages which is again on the agenda of the CMI.

The fact that ship's value has a bearing on the salvage remuneration is explained in Chapter 10. The English method of assessing ship's value "with commitments" plays an important role outside England also because of the many arbitration awards in salvage cases delivered in London. I once again marshal my arguments against this concept. The "increased value" owing to a charterparty will not pass to the salvors if the ship is sold to satisfy their claim unless the seller and the buyer agree. The charterparty and the vessel are not legally one and the same unit. Why should only a high rate charterparty be made to increase ship's value but the low rate charterparty not go to reduce that value? Why is it that only a charterparty should be taken into account but not other types of contract, say the long term bunkering contract that may well have an important impact on the economic result. Why is the encouragement to salvors regarded as a valid argument for the "with commitment" concept as the salvage industry elsewhere is not dependent on that indirect form of support? International uniformity, the goal of the Salvage Convention, is made more difficult to obtain because of the English valuation method. This is the gist of the arguments advanced.

Chapter 11 on general average shows the difficulties that meet the average adjuster in assessing ship's value for general average purposes, (i) when there are market restrictions, (ii) where a ship is so badly damaged that it is hardly feasible to bring her from a small place to a port that has repair facilities, (iii) where the end of the voyage comes immediately after a political or economic event that has a bearing on *inter alia* tonnage values. An amendment introduced in the York/Antwerp Rules 1974 makes the rules explicitly say, in Rule XVII, that neither the beneficial nor detrimental commitments should be taken into account in assessing ship's value.

In Chapter 12 on limitation of liability I use as an example the vessel *Eve* in order to show the amount of her limited liability according to the tonnage rule of the 1976 Convention and the *fortune de mer* system of the USA and also some of the problems in respect of ship's value in this connection. I add some comments on the merits of the two systems.

Conclusions

None of the models or methods described in the text can be adopted as the only correct one for assessing ship's value in all situations. No prize can be distributed for "the first opened correct answer" in respect of valuation methods. The analyses made in the various sections show unmistakably, however, that the *market value* is the most useful method for arriving at a satisfactory and proper result. The objectivity in the valuation is maintained as against the subjective element that goes with the others. Where the *market value* cannot be used one will have to resort to some other method and the *replacement value* is then probably the next best. The valuation of ships being no exact science it may sometimes be necessary to use a combination of several methods to arrive at the true value of the ship.

I was not sure when embarking on this study whether the purpose for which the valuation is made was of any importance for the method to be used. The investigations made show that the answer is no. Perhaps one should add the qualification that for salvage and general average it is ship's value in damaged condition that counts.

In the sections on ship's value for credit purposes, on collision recovery and on salvage I have explained at some length my arguments against using ship's value "with commitments" rather than as a free ship. In the summary I have reproduced the gist of the reasons for this attitude. Of course I note with satisfaction that the concept of the free ship is now part of the York/Antwerp Rules 1974 dealing with general average. Suffice it to say here that assessing ship's value "with commitments" rather than as a free ship appears as erroneous from a theoretical point of view as it is unfortunate for its practical consequences.

Bibliography

Ameln, H, Jr: *Håndbok i Praktisk Sjørett* (Oslo 1955).

Arnold: *Law of Marine Insurance and Average*, Vols I and II, 16th edn., by M Mustill and J C B Gilman (London 1961).

Association of Average Adjusters of the United States: *Reports* 1948 and 1960.

Association International de Dispacheurs Européens: *Report 10th Assembly 1979* (Cambridge), quoted as AIDE Cambridge.

Benedict, E C: *The Law of American Admiralty* (7th edn.).

Bengtsson, B: *Försäkringsrätt* (Stockholm 1973).

Berlingieri, G: *Assistenza e Salvataggio nella Navigazione Marittima, Interna e Aerea Ricupero e Ritrovamento* (Genova 1968).

Berning, J: *Omsetningsformue som kreditsikring* (Copenhagen 1973).

Braekhus, S: *Bergning* (Oslo 1967).

Braekhus, S: *Kontraktspant i skip* (1956); republished in *Juridiske Arbeiden for Sø och Land* (Oslo 1968).

Braekhus, S and A Rein: *Håndbok i P & I Forsikring* (Arendal 1979).

Buglass, L J: *Marine Insurance and General Average in the United States: An Average Adjuster's Viewpoint* (Cambridge, Maryland 1973).

Cargo Insurance and Modern Transport Ed. by K Grönfors (1970: 3).

Carver: *Carriage of Goods by Sea*, 13th edn., (London 1982).

Clarus: *Notes on Marine Insurance Practice* (London 1932).

Danielsson, E: *Några anmärkningar till 35 kap. 5 § Rättegångsbalken* (Stockholm 1953). Del av Försäkrings-Juridiska Föreningens Publikation No. 10.

Dover, V: *Analysis of Marine Insurance Clauses* (London 1956).

Drachman Bentzon, A og K Christensen: *Lov om Forsikringsavtaler*, 2nd edn. (Copenhagan 1962).

Droit Maritime Comparé: Vols 1–40.

Le Droit Maritime Francais.

Dymling, P: *Haagreglerna och kyltransporter* (1969: 4).

Falkanger, T: *Lossing og bortskaffelse av last som er sterkt beskadiget* (1972).

Federspiel, H: *Begrebet Interesse i Laeren om Forsikring* (Copenhagen 1901).

Flodhammar, G: *Tvångsinlösning av aktier* (Sv J T 1971).

Gilmore & Black: *The Law of Admiralty* (Brooklyn 1957).

Gorton, L: *The Concept of the Common Carrier in Anglo-American law* (1971).

Grönfors, K: *Trafikskadeansvar utanför kontraktsförhållanden* (Stockholm 1952). (Quoted as Trafikskadeansvar.)

——: "Agande och Brukande som Kreditunderlag", *Nordisk Gjenklang, Festskrift til Carl Jacob Arnholm* (Oslo 1969). (Quoted as Ägande och Brukande.)

——: "Sjörättens Kollisionsansvar", *Arkiv for Sjørett*, Vol. 12 1975, p. 327.

——: *Transporträttsliga studier* (1975).

——: *Tidsfaktorn vid transportavtal* (1974).

Grundt, Th: *Laerebok i Norsk Forsikringsrett* (Oslo 1939).

Hagberg, J: *Enforced Sales of Vessels, Vol. II in the Maritime Law series of the International Bar Association* (December 1977).

Hasselrot, P: *York Antwerpen Reglerna 1924. En handbok om gemensamt haveri* (Stockholm 1928).

Healy, N J: *The New York Produce Exchange Time Charter* (1975).

Healy, N J and D J Sharpe: *Cases and Materials on Admiralty* (St Paul, Minn 1974).

Hellner, J: *Föräkringsrätt*, 2nd edn. (Lund 1965).

——: *Skadeståndsrätt*, 4th edn. (Stockholm 1985).

Hernmark, M: *Lösekilling vid expropriation för tätbebyggelse*, 3rd edn. (Stockholm 1967).

Hughes, R M: *Handbook of Admiraty Law* (St Paul, Minn 1920).

Hull Claims Analysis, Vol. I, Issues Nos 2 and 5 1984. "Ships values in cases of salvage and general average; Ship values—an anomaly? Future—is there a third alternative?"

Hult, Ph: *Bidrag till läran om Fösäkring av Tredje mans intresse* (Stockholm 1927).

——: *Förläningar om Försäkringsavtalen* (Stockholm 1936).

Hurd, H B: *The Law and Practice of Marine Insurance relating to Collision Damages and other liabilities to Third Parties*, 2nd edn. (London 1952).

Jacobs, V: *Le Droit Maritime Belge. Commentaire de la loi du 21 août 1879*, Tome l (Bruxelles 1889).

James, Ph H: *Introduction to English Law*, 6th edn. (1966).

de Juglart, M & J Villeneau: *Répertoire Méthodique et Pratique de L'Assistance en mer* (Paris 1962).

Jørgensen, Ph, Pr Lyngsø & H Tranov: *Dansk Forsikringsret*, 1 *Almindelig Del*, (Copenhagen 1965).

Kačic, H: *Naknada Stete u Slučaju Pomorskih Brodova* (Zagreb 1968).

Karlgren, Hj: *Skadeståandsrätten* (Lund 1943).

Kleiven, I: "Kollisionsansvar og regress", *Arkiv for Sjørett*, Vol. II 1972, p. 489.

Kennedy W R: *A Treatise on the Law of Civil Salvage*, 4th edn. (London 1958).

Kofoed, E & E Aagaard-Hansen: *Sø-og anden transportforsikring* (Odense 1971).

Ljungholm C: *Beränkning av expropriationsersättning* (Sv J T 1944).

Lureau, P: *Commentaires des Polices Francaises d'Assurances Maritimes sur Corps de Navires* (Paris 1974); see also under Rodière below.

Marsden: *The Law of Collision at Sea*, 11th edn., by K G McGuffie (London 1961).

Modern transport and sales financing, Ed. by K Grönfors (1974).

Mustill, M J: *Pseudo-demurrage and the arrived ship* (1974).

Nolst Trenité, J G L: *Zeeverzekering*, 2nd edn. (Haarlem 1928).

Norris, M J: *The Law of Salvage* (Mount Kisco, New York 1958).

Parenthou, R: "La Valeur des navires et l'avarie commune", *Droit Maritime Français*, 1979, p. 131.

Persson, U: *Skada och Värde* (Lund 1953).

——: *Skadestånds-och Förskringsrättsliga Studier* (Lund 1962). (Quoted as "Studier.")

Pineus, K: *General Average. The Practical Problems* (Gothenburg 1985).

——: *Le Droit maritime suédois* (1971).

——: *Ship's Value* (1975).

Pineus, K and G Röhreke: *Limited Liability in Collision Cases* (London 1984).

Platou, O: *Søret* (Oslo 1900).

Prüssman, H: *Seehandelsrecht* (Munich 1968).

Rahmn, L: *Skadeståndsberäkning vid fartygssammanstötning*; Papers presented before the Nordic Maritime Seminar in Mariehamn 1976.

Ramberg, J: *Cancellation of contracts of affreightment on account of war and similar circumstances* (1970: 2).

Ripert, G: *Droit Maritime*, 4th edn., Vols. I–III (Paris 1950–1953).

Riska, O: *Om försäkring av Driftsintresse i Sjöfart* (Helsingfors 1964).

Ritter, C: *Das Recht der Seeversicherung*, 2nd edn., (Hamburg 1967).

Robinson, G H: *Handbook of Admiralty Law in the United States* (St Paul, Minn 1939).

Rodière, R: *Traité Général de Droit Maritime, Evénements de Mer* (Paris 1972), with the co-operation of P Lureau.

Rodhe, K: *Lärobok i Obligationsrätt*, 2nd edn. (Stockholm 1969).

Roscoe, E S: *The Measure of Damages in Maritime Collisions*, 3rd edn. (London 1939).

Rune, Chr: *Rätt till Skepp. Sjörättsföreningen i Göteborg*. Skriftserie No. 55 (Gothenburg 1976).

Saga, P: Aspects juridiques de la définition des navires en droit libanais, en droit comparé et en droit international, *Droit Maritime Français*, 1976, p. 366.

Schadee, H: *The draft maritime code of the Netherlands* (1973).

Schaps-Abraham: *Das Deutsche Seerecht*, 2nd edn. (Berlin 1962).

Schimmering, W: *Bergung und Hilfsleitung im Seerecht und Seeversicherungsrecht*, (Karlsruhe 1971).

Schiørring, Geo K: *Den Danske Søforsikringspolice* (Copenhagen 1924).

Selmer, K S: *Laerebok i Forsikringsrett*, Bind I (Oslo 1973).

Selvig, E: *Erstatningsberegning ved lasterskade*. Handelshögskolans i Göteborg skrifter (1962).

———: *Om container-konossement og remburs* (1970: 7).

Sindballe, Kr: *Dansk Forsikringsret Første Del* (Copenhagen 1948).

Sisula, L: *Containerklausulen i Haag-Visby-Reglerna* (1970: 1).

Smeesters, C & G: *Droit Maritime et Droit Fluviale* (Brussels 1929).

Sotiropoulos, P R: *Die Beschränkung der Reederhaftung* (Berlin 1962).

Sutton, Ch T: *The Assessing of Salvage Awards* (London 1949).

Thorbjørnsen, Kr: *No Cure—No Pay* (Oslo 1951).

Tiberg, H: *Kreditsäkerheten i fartyg* (Stockholm 1968).

———: *Bailees' and Lessees' Protection against Third Parties under Swedish Law* (Stockholm 1965).

Tyberg, N: *Om Søassuradørens Ansvar* (Copenhagen 1952).

———: *Dansk Søforsikrings-Konvention af 2 April 1934. Udgivet af N Tybjerg med noter og sagregister*, 2nd edn. (Copenhagen 1963).

Welinder, C: *Skatterättens värderingsregler* (Stockholm 1949).

Wetterstein, P: *Globalbegränsning av sjörättsligt skadestånd. En skadeståndsrättslig studie* (Åbo 1980).

Index*

age of vessel, considerations of,
23–24
AIDE Conference, Cambridge
(1978),
Working Report, 110 and n
assessment "with commitments" or
as "free ship", 35

Banker's view of ship finance (F W
Arnesen), *quoted*, 53–54, 58n
bibliography, 119–122
Buglass on general average, *quoted*,
102

cargo space, 26
certificate of valuation, *example of*,
22–23
challenge for fraudulent action, 65n
charterparty,
influence on ship's value,
considerations, 34
in England, 39–43
outside England, 37–39
situation in the USA, 44–45
profitable and unprofitable,
examples of, 34–35
provisions of, taking into
account, 33
registration of, in Norway, 52
sale of ship, 45–46 and n
claims secured by lien (silent
rights), 33n
Classification Regulations, Lloyd's
Register of Shipping (806), 24n
Classification Societies and surveys,
24–25
CMI Assembly (1986), draft rules,
86
CMI Conference (Athens, 1962),
on measure of damages in
collision cases, 78–80

CMI Conference—*cont.*
on registration of charterparty,
50
CMIH Conference (Hamburg,
1974), 101
collision loss, claim against
counterparty, 75–86
collision recovery, relevant time,
17–18
commodity shipment, value, 8
company law, incidence of, 19
company liquidation value as
applied to a vessel, 12–13
constructive total loss, 59 and n
continuous surveys, 24–25
Convention limitation systems,
USA and 1976 systems,
compared, 111–114
Convention on Collision (1910) Art
3, 75n
Convention on Limitation of
Liability for Maritime Claims
(1976), 64 and n
counterparty, claim against,
collision loss, 75–86
credit purposes, value for, 16–17
cross-examination of expert
witnesses, 30–31

damaged condition value, 28
demarcation lines, 6–7
demurrage claims, 81 and n
discounted future earning power,
10 and n
discrepancy, agreed value insured/
actual value, in total loss case,
64–74
distribution of recovery, 81–83
dividend value, 9
liquidation value in relation to
open policy, and, 68
dual valuation, 60 and n, 61

economic depression and cost of
replacement, 11
English method/collision claim
valuation, *discussion of*, 36,
83–84
evidence, oral/written, 20
expectation value, 10, 55

Fairplay's actual usage periods for
various kinds of vessels, 29
Finance and the future of the supertanker
(B S Douglas), *quoted*, 54
Financing an expanding fleet (G A
Newell), *quoted*, 54
financing of ships, credit ceilings,
54n, 55n
fluctuations in value, *example*, 15
fraudulent action, 65n
future earnings, assessing, 10
future expenditure, assessing, 10

general average, 101–110
General Average (E W Congdon),
quoted, 101–102
general market value, surplus/
shortage of empty tonnage,
28–31
geography, influence on value for
general average, 104–105
German Democratic Republic,
Festpreise, 32 and n
"going concern", value to owner as,
83

Hudson, N G, Chairman,
Association of Average
Adjusters, *quoted*, 99
hull insurance, 56–74
open/valued policy, meaning, 57
value at inception of risk and the
time element, 16
what is covered by, 58–59
hull interest/freight interest/
disbursements,
insurance, 61–64

inflation and cost of replacement,
11
insurable value, definitions,
Maritime Insurance Act 1906, 56
Swedish Marine Insurance Plan
(Art. 27), 56

Japan,
licensed valuers in, 29 and n
stages in assessing value for
collision, salvage or general
average, 29

Kennedy, W R, on value, *quoted*, 41
and n

leasing of ships, 43n
liability, limitation of, tonnage rule,
111–114
limitation of liability, 111–114
fortune de mer, 19 and n
tonnage rule, 111–114
uniformity of rules of, 111
USA system, 64
Lloyd's Form of Salvage Agreement
(the LOF), *extracts from*, 96
Lloyd's Register of Statistical
Tables (1972), *quoted*, 36
loading and discharging gear, 26
loss of profit claims, 80–81
loss, total, unvalued or open policy,
67 and n

Maritime Arbitration Commission
(MAC), USSR Chamber of
Trade & Industry, *quoted*, 88
Maritime Insurance Act 1906,
insurable value, definition of,
56
*Market Conditions and the Availability
of Money* (B Quick), *quoted*, 54
market trend, influence of, 29
market value, 22–33
generally, 7–9
in controlled economy, 8
in free or mixed economy, 8
method of valuation, merits of,
117
measure of damages in collision
cases,
British Maritime Association
and, 78
CMI Conference (1962) and,
78–80
general discussion of, 75–77
Maritime Association of the
Federal Republic of
Germany, *quoted*, 79

Swedish Association of
    International Maritime
    Law, *quoted*, 79
vessels of special character, 78
merchant fleet statistics,
    1973 (G H Dodsworth), 36
    1985, *comments on*, 37

newbuilding construction prices,
    contractual clauses and
    delivery time, 26–27
Nordic Average Adjustors Meeting,
    Helsingfors (1954), translation
    of minutes, 103–104
Norwegian Insurance Plan (Arts.
    158, 160, 223), 63 and n

official enactments, effect on value,
    32
oil,
    bunker/diesel, cost of, 26n
    consumption factors, 25–26
open policy, market and utility
    value, *discussed*, 71

Package deals and syndicates (G H
    Dodsworth), *quoted*, 54
political blacklisting, 29n
propulsion, mode of, 25

reduced usefulness of vessel,
    discussed, 70
refrigerating machinery, 26
registration of charterparties,
    conference discussion of, 50–51
removal to port of repair, cost, 108
repairs, time element, 92
replacement value,
    factors affecting, 10–11
    market value as alternative to,
    117
restitutio in integrum theory, 17
restricted market, effect on value,
    31–33

Salvage, 87–100
    Beyer on relevance of charter, 38
    chartered vessels and, 38, 94
    English valuation method,
    97–100
    "free of charter" value (Braekhus
    on), 37

general average, and relevant
    time, 19
London cases, statistics, 96–97
    and n
pragmatic approach to, 87–88
The Stigstad case, 38
valuation, method of, 100
value in relation to, 13 and n
Salvage Convention (Art. 8), 87
salved value, importance of, 88–89
salvor's lien, 99
Scandinavian Insurance Acts, 56n
scrap value, 109 and n
Scrutton, L J, *quoted* on value, 41
Seatrade Money and Ship's
    Conferences (1973/1974), 53,
    98n
selling value as basis for loss claim,
    13 and n
shipbrokers, role of, 20–21
shipbuilding, economic aspects, 47
shipping partnership incidence of,
    19
ship's value,
    as a claim against counterparty
        in case of loss owing to
        collision, 75–86
    assessment of, practical
        approach, 20–21
    for credit purposes, 47–55
    introduction to study, 1–5
    summary and conclusions, 115–
        118
size (tonnage and carrying
    capacity), considerations, 23
specialized vessels,
    market value, and, 94
    valuing, 27–28
speed, factors relating to, 25 and n
standardized depreciation, 11
steel ships, special surveys of, 24n
subjective value, 83
Swedish Act on Damages (1972),
    quoted, 75
Swedish Insurance Act (Art. 37),
    quoted and *discussed*, 17, 68–71
Swedish Insurance Plan (Art. 124),
    quoted, 82–83
Swedish Marine Insurance Plan
    (Art. 27),
    hull interest, definition, 62
    insurable value, definition, 56

Swedish Maritime Board (Art. 15), *quoted*, 37
Swedish Maritime Code (to 1967), cases under, 105–108
Swedish Maritime Law Committee, and assessment of value, 13
survival of charterparty, discussion on, 51–53
Swedish State Fund for Small Tonnage, 54n

tax law, incidence of, 19
The New Yorker (13 May 1974) on ship's life spans, *quoted*, 24n
time element, 15–19
time factor, end of adventure, 109 110
time, relevance of in assessing value, 15–16
total loss/unvalued or open policy, and dividend value, 68
and liquidation value, 68
and market/utility value, 71–74
and Swedish Marine Insurance Plan, 68–70
trend of the market, 29
type of vessel, relevance, 23

unvalued or open policy, 67–74
usefulness, reduced, *discussed*, 70
utility value, basis for credit, as, 53, 55
construction factors, and, 12 and n

valuation, certificates, obtaining, 20
credit purposes, for, 48–50
hindsight, not to be used in making, 22n

influence of purpose on method, 117
methods, *discussed*, 84–85
time, extraneous factors of, not to be used in, 22n
value, after salvage, pragmatic approach, 89–91
for credit purposes, 13 and n
for insurance purposes (*Richter quoted*), 57n
of salvaged ships, assessing, legal views, 92–94
valued policy elements, 57–60
valuers, opinions, conflicting, resolution of, 21 and n
status of, 20n
values in general, 6–14
vessel, obsolete, replacement cost refused, 10
off beaten track, 30n
of specialized design, 10
voyage's end, disrupted market, effect of, 103–105
termination of venture, 109–110
value at destination (Swedish cases), 105–108
vessel removed or immobilized, 108–109

wear and tear, deductions for, 11 and n

York/Antwerp Rules (1974), generally, 98–9
Rule XVII *quoted*, 101